LIFE WON'T
BE
PERFECT...

BY MELVINA W.

LET IT Go

LET IT

Copyright © 2025 Melvina Washington

Self Publishing Services provided by Krystal Lee Enterprises LLC (KLE Publishing)

All rights reserved. No parts of this book may be reproduced, distributed, or used in any manner, including photocopying, recording, or other electronic or mechanical methods without the prior written permission of the copywriter owner, except for the use of brief quotations in a book review and certain noncommercial uses permitted by copyright law.

Paperback: 978-1-945066-74-0

Please send comments and questions for Publishing to:
Krystal Lee Enterprises
sales@KLEPub.com

To Reach the Author:
Email: info@IAmMelvina.com

Web: IAMMelvina.com
Contact: Phone: 815-635-8462
Printed in the United States of America.

Disclaimers
The information in this book was correct at the time of publication, but the Author does not assume any liability for loss or damage caused by errors or omissions. These are my memories, from my perspective, and I have tried to represent events as faithfully as possible.

Dedication

For my lover, my best friend, the only man of my life, my husband Glenn

For my three grown daughters, who I love unconditionally and forever will until I die, Mariama, Sierra, and Amira

For my parents who taught me love, gave me love, and I have loved since the beginning of time, Melvin and Albertha

And to you, the reader, believe in yourself, dreams big, works hard, plays harder, and TRULY believe in infinite possibilities. You need to make things happen "Come Hell or High Water," and if it is not what you want anymore, "Let It Go!"

"I Didn't Say it Was Over!"

-This book is for YOU!

Table of Contents

Introduction	7
Let it Go!	11
Don't Let Go of Your Dreams	23
What the Hell Happened?	45
Financial Planning	69
When They Say No	91
Release Passion	111
Let Go of Judgment	129
When You Are Not Appreciated	157
Over Analyzing - It Will Never Get Done	179
There Is No Perfection	211
About Melvina Washington	217

INTRODUCTION

LET IT *Go*

Introduction

So, how have you been? I trust you have gotten to the point in your life where you have decided you were going to make it Come Hell or High Water–or have you not? What is going on if you are in book three and are still not convinced that your mindset is your best asset? If your mind can point to your dreams, why don't you still have them?

Before you come up with excuses, I am going to stop you. You can't tell me it is because you are fat, black, have a disability, got children, a husband, grew up in poverty, or that you got made fun of as a child. Check out the book, "I Didn't Say It Was Over," all that is my life story, too. If you read book number two, you know that I am a black woman with a flat ass that my husband loves. I am a woman with three girls born with different disabilities and challenges.

I was born with a nerve loss that makes me legally deaf, and I passed that trait to two of my daughters - the twins. I grew up in the South, where being black–especially being dark, was a challenge all by itself. To be big or chunky, my entire upbringing did not make life easy for me. I knew I was beautiful because my parents told me so, but that still didn't shield me from the pain I felt as a child.

I learned early on that my parents couldn't protect me no matter how badly they wanted to. I had to learn to defend myself. I came out of the corner that I was balled up in too many times crying. I came out swinging with confidence, and I didn't look back. I wasn't totally confident in my abilities, but I realized I couldn't show my fear.

I needed to get scrappy and find solutions, not point to my problems. I learned that money was the equalizer. Success is something that doesn't care about my skin color. My body type. Or any other thing I was prematurely judged on as a youth.

I realized–and I want to help you see, too–you got to get to a point where you let it go! And I mean it. You gotta "Let it Go!" The more you try to hold on to old experiences, fears, and concerns or think pleasing others will somehow make you happy, the more you will be sadly mistaken. You are going to want to fight, but there will be nowhere to turn but to yourself.

So spare yourself the trouble and start thinking about what matters right now. You need to focus on what you can change and everything else, especially what you are waiting on others to do; you may have to Let it Go.

Introduction

I know I talk loud and fast; another negative some may say I have is that I turned into a win. I use my personality daily, and I have learned to embrace all my ways. I am grateful that I have a husband that loves every part of me–even with my disfigured flat-dimpled-up butt.

On my 50th, I took a nude photoshoot because I am "freeeeeeeee" and when I say I am free, I mean do what I want, say what I feel, and how I feel. As you get older, you better master how to let things go! Nobody has time for stroking out because of stress or being depressed about stuff that others don't want to change. Some people enjoy seeing you in pain because it makes them feel better about their pain. And you learn that time waits for no one…

I have so much to share in this book, and right now, we are merely at the tip of the iceberg shown in book one, Come Hell or High Water, and I Didn't Say It Was Over. Let's pull back the curtain and talk about it all—family, love, sex, business, career, money, and our future. If you are down, keep turning the pages with me, Melvina.

Don't know who I am? Check the QR, and let's get to work! Keep with me because I gotta' a whole lot mo' to share with you. I didn't say it was over; we bout' to Let it Go!

Let it Go!

I know ya'll know me quite well by now. You know that I love three things, not in a particular order, but Love, Family, and Money. I know the three things that need to work together to make me happy and afford the life I want to live and share with my family. I learned these three things that motivate me early, which has helped me persevere to get to this point.

But it hasn't been peaches and cream, and I have not gotten everything I want out of life–yet! So what have I accomplished, and what remains to be had for my life? It hasn't always been a bumpy road for me. I grew up in an amazing family with two parents and my brother; I'm the oldest, which might explain a lot.

I took heavily after my father, and I make no apologies for being like him. My mom probably wanted me to take on more of her traits, but that wasn't me. I think like my dad, talk like him, joke like him, and like him, I don't know a stranger. He has greatly influenced

Melvina W.

my life, and I love him dearly.

Now, that doesn't mean I don't have a lot of respect and love for my mother. She has been a cornerstone in helping me to become a wife, mother, and the woman I am today. Growing up in the South with three strikes working against me wasn't easy. I have dark skin, always had some meat on my bones, and I was born legally deaf due to a nerve loss. I don't say all this for you to feel sorry for me and think, oh, poor me - poor baby…naww!

I am doing fine, but there were some dark moments when I wanted to ball up in a corner and cry. Sometimes in school, I did self-isolate and hide in a corner, but that didn't stop the racist nicknames and jokes. My mom pulled me to the side a few times and built up my confidence by reminding me how the world can treat people. Children are children, so it wasn't necessarily because they were evil children; some of those children I have met as adults and they share their remorse for how they treated me.

I don't hold any guilt for what they did or the things they said. When I was young, of course, it hurt, and I still deal with some of the opinions that have been formed today. You know that doesn't last long because I am Melvina! I am not perfect, but I know I am valuable. My father made sure I knew that, and so did my mother. My nuclear family was one I have always been grateful to have.

My brother and I were close growing up but lived different lives. He made choices I did not, and in

Let it Go!

life, that happens. I had to watch him make some very sketchy choices that I would never make, but in the end, I had to let it go. Sometimes, we can want to change people more than they want to. I will talk more about this later because I know you have a family member, and if you are honest, it is time for you to let it go.

More about me before I open this can of worms is I am happily married with three daughters. I love my husband and know he loves and is in love with me. I know for some of y'all out there, people have tried to separate the meaning of the two, and although I get it, I feel it can be a crock of BS. You either love me or you don't. You either like me, or you don't. What the hell is all this business about? Love you but not in love with you?

People need to let it go and just be honest, dang! Let me put that lid on for a minute because you know I am gonna circle back to relationships. I have seen too much going on in the world happening with women my age. Yes, we all have a past and need to determine how we want to move forward. Some people, you gotta cut off and not look back! Then, there are those you have to buckle down and build with. You have to know a good thing when you have it, and I know I have that with Glenn.

Meeting my husband, Glenn, you can learn more in "Come Hell or High Water," my first book, where I talk about how we met. In "I Didn't Say It Was Over," I talk more about how we kept the flame burning in our relationship. In this book you are reading, "Let It Go," I have to tell you how we keep sex fun and how to keep people out of your business, and I am talking about noisy family members and those with an opinion. I haven't talked as much about those who will judge how you and your Boo do your thing, but I want to let it go and let you know it's time to stop living under a magnifying glass.

I know that when you live your life, and others look on, they all develop opinions. Some will try and say how wrong you are for what you choose to do. They will try to second-guess your decisions or viewpoint but don't let them do that to you. You will make mistakes, they will make mistakes, you won't be perfect, and they won't be perfect. If you were expecting perfection, or they were, both of you need to Let it Go!!

I wrote the first two books because I started my journey in life as a wife with a great example. My parents showed me how to work with someone and be myself. Being with my husband for nearly thirty years has not always been easy. We got to rough patches like anyone, but we had to see the big picture and let go of all the things that could pull us apart. Not to say we didn't talk about things and work them out, but we don't hold grudges against one another. We have to allow each other to be ourselves and choose to be together on things.

Marrying him was the best thing I ever did, but there is one thing I question if we should still do. I am going to tell you that later, of course; that's new information. About my life, I raised three beautiful girls with Glenn. They are all college graduates, out of my house, and making a life for themselves. They all had their own challenges in life that they had to overcome, and

Let it Go!

their challenges were not an excuse to NOT achieve everything necessary for them to take care of themselves.

I taught our girls that they had to be able to take care of themselves. They needed to know that their medical challenges did not exempt them from trying their best, getting an education, and becoming self-sufficient. I fought for my daughters at the school level and in life to be solid, confident, and know they are loved. Glenn and I are so proud of what we did for them, but if you close enough, you can see how we may have failed them they would argue.

I would never tell you I am a perfect wife or mother, but I gave nothing but my best. What I knew and didn't, I went out and learned and gave them all I had. I will never be guilty of holding back from them what I knew I could give. Sometimes, your best is not enough, and people can demand more of you. They can say what you have done falls short of their expectations and penalize you for being human and making mistakes.

I believe in taking ownership of your mistakes, but I would never tell anyone to stay under someone's shoes and wait for them to let you come up when they are ready. For some of us, we would wait until forever and still not get up. There will be things you are going to have to let go! I am not saying abandon anybody you shouldn't, but I do believe in boundaries, and I want to share more about that later.

So I told you about my love, my family–and yes, there are more people I love and who are like

Melvina W.

family to me, you can find them in the other two books, but what about money? Ching, ching! I am not shy about my love for money, and if you think your discomfort with money will wear off on me, you are certainly wrong. I do believe money solves problems. I think everybody needs it, and some of us need or want it more than others. I have things I want out of life, and I am not afraid to work for it!

I feel like if I worked for it, I should be able to enjoy it. So I eat my cake and ice cream, too! Don't tell my personal trainer this; they always take the fun out of life. I have always loved food, but it doesn't make my top three.

I chose money because I use it as a tool, and it is a main resource for creating your happiness. And what I mean is I couldn't pay off my daughter's education without it. I couldn't buy them all cars at 16 or keep us living in a house that is paid for without it.

I have been financially smart with money because I know I am building a future for my family and those who I love and care for. I think being a good mother is more than listening to people bitch and complain about things but also about showing your love and appreciation in how others provide and look out for them. I know all my flaws. You can find a smudge or imperfection if you look at a glass long enough. However, one thing is for sure: my heart and intentions will always be pure.

I will talk more about that because I have to. Fake people, as you get older, you learn to have less

Let it Go!

and less room for them in your life. I have no problem with letting people go. You are not going to make everyone happy anyway, so find your own peace.

I was talking about money, wasn't I? Now, this money thing, I am a medical coder and not a medical biller. I don't do anything with insurance. I do not demand money, although that part doesn't sound half bad, for medical expenses. My job as a coder is to code services for the hospitals and/or doctor offices for the bills to be created for the patients and the insurance companies to get money - it also tells the story of the patient's care at that facility by the codes we used. To put it in layman's terms, for patients in hospitals, coders code the services received by reading the chart to create bills for reimbursement from the insurance company or for the patient to pay. So, medical coders are after the money!

I started in the IT field, and I fell in love when I came upon this niche. I knew I had to work it, and it wouldn't just be given to me. I was a black woman entering a field heavily dominated by white men or white women. I do not fit the bill statistically, but I became a winning medical coder and have steadily built a name for myself that I rather enjoy. Today, I help train medical coders, source jobs for licensed coders, and mentor coders on how to elevate on their current jobs to stay employed or make more.

I started making entry money, and it steadily rose from about 40k to 50k, 70k, and then over 100k. I found a system, and I started to teach others when the work didn't stop flowing. When you are great at what you do, and you build connections to help things keep moving, there is nothing you cannot achieve. I started this business with no connections, but I was intentional about meeting people in this field and winning.

No matter what hand you have been dealt in life, I can show you how to win with it in medical coding and life! I had to write this third book, "Let it Go," because I have seen too many women get held back from reaching success because of fear, poor planning, listening to the wrong people, overanalyzing, and not enjoying the good things in front of them. Life is short, you have to make the best of it and live it how you want to.

If you don't like how much you make, you want to travel, shop more, or whatever, decide to change it. You will not change anything by holding on to what keeps you stuck. We have to let it go and allow ourselves to get what we want out of life. If you are picking up what I am putting down, you need to turn the pages and reach the end of this book.

I am the same Melvina in all three of my books, and I am so proud of this trilogy that shares key information for medical coders, women, and those looking to change their lives. If you were thinking you can't, know that believing you can is enough to start the process. I didn't think I would have my own business someday, but I do! Running Infinity HIM, my medical coding school and service company, I have put tons of people to work. Finding what makes you happy can be a good thing and bring new options to your life.

Let it Go!

I know I have started on other journeys because I believe in business; you can never have too much of a good thing, such as money. I started a woman's company, Infinite Beauty and I have a podcast titled, "Give Me Something to Work With." I named my show because I feel like whatever you want to accomplish in life, you have to put something out there to get it. Nothing is going to fall in your life. You have to give people something to work with! Hell, you even have to give yourself something to work with!

I wanted to have my published books and continue to work with my publisher. She gave me something to work with, and now, I want to do more to help people. I talk about money, but I have a heart, and I love volunteering and giving back through my sorority, Zeta Phi Beta Sorority, Inc. I do believe in balancing your life and not throwing everything we might not like, or that challenges us out the window. This book will not promote that kind of thinking, but it will point to looking at what you think. How do you feel about your life right now?

Are you at a point where you are ready to do something new or to live life differently? As I got older, I got more serious about what I wanted. It is time to get serious about what you want because no one will value what you want more than you do. You have to see that you first have value before you trust others to attribute or recognize it in you. When I didn't know my value, I accepted anything. That had to change, and the moment it did in grade school, I never looked back and only saw my life as a steady elevation. I believe that good things should be mine, and they have been.

Melvina W.

You can speak your life and get what you want. My dad had an " it's my way or the highway" mode of operation, and in many ways, I do, too. It's not that I won't hear you out, but I am not following no one that can't lead me to where I want to be. So, if you feel like I do, and you want what I'm putting down, let's go. I have a whole lotta mo.

Let it Go!

Don't Let Your Dreams Go!

You like what I am putting down, so why is it not you? Please don't tell me you are picking up this third book of mine and still not ready to let people go? I know some things in this book might make you share a tear, temporarily, but you're going to be alright. People will always have an opinion, and we cannot let how others feel about our lives to impact how we treat ourselves.

I remember when I first shared my vision for life with my parents. Although they did laugh when I said I would have a maid and a driver. They thought, why would that be necessary? Can't you just cook, clean, and drive yourself? "Yes, I can, but I don't want to."

For some of us, we have allowed moments like this to block our dreams. My dream is not to cook, clean, and be a stay-at-home wife like my mother. Although I love her dearly, she and I never wanted the same things out of life in this regard. I want to be free to make money, to travel, and to be happy on my terms. Some people in your life mean you no harm, but they want you to be happy on terms they can identify with.

My parents didn't understand what I was saying as a ten and thirteen-year-old girl, but I was never confused. I have always known what my dream was and what it is still today. If you are not clear about what you want out of life, now is the time to get clear about it. I was free as a child to dream, and I thank my parents for that. And of course, I am even more freer now to dream and make it a reality. Trust me, I didn't say this was over, I know to let it go.

My dad has always encouraged me to be the best I could be. For me to be my best means these things need to be taken care of why I do what I am called to do. If I was sitting around doing what others wanted me to do, I would be broke and very unhappy. If you are living the outcome of other people's plans for you, you probably are broke and unhappy. And trust me, you get nowhere with that thought process - sitting around waiting on others, listening to them, etc. I know, and I believe you know as well - that doesn't work.

I have helped too many medical coders shift their mindset from being locked in on what others want for them to helping them drill down on what they want for themselves. Yes, doing what makes everyone else comfortable might make sense and make their life easier. They don't mind seeing you struggle in ways they feel are normal.

Most people, I feel, are used to suffering more

than being happy. I think this has something to do with being accepted by your surroundings or people. For me, I push fear and step out on faith or what I like to say is that Christian thing.

Well, I am not a Christian. I tell this to Dr. Lee all the time. I don't see how being poor could be what God wants for me. I don't see why struggling and not being able to pay Peter or Paul is a good thing. I am not here to argue religion. I believe in God, but I am not a Christian. I believe that God wants me better and for all of us to live our lives to the fullest and step out on faith, for real!

I believe we should NOT use anything to hold us back from what we want to achieve in life. If you find that you have plateaued, it is because you keep bending to everyone else's expectations of you. Have you reached a stage in your life yet where you are tired of bending for people and life events to kick you in the butt? Are you tired yet?

I presume your answer is "yes," otherwise, why would you grab my book? I am here to help you remember your why and get back to the fundamental basics of what you want out of life. When we get lost in outer space, it is because we have lost track of what we are pursuing. We are no longer focused on the road ahead because we are too busy looking behind us worried about everyone else.

I have a question to ask you. What has being worried about everyone else done for you? Do the people you stop your dreams for, come and check on you?

Do they come and pay your bills if you can't do it? Do they put in on the rent, buy you the stuff you like, cut your grass, and help you take care of business?

Then why are you listening to any of them? Why are you worried about how they will feel about you charging them something to be in your space? Yes, if people want to put in on my dreams, they are going to have to Give Me Something To Work With! I made that the title of my podcast for a reason. I am not going to stop my dreams for someone else's.

People are quick to give their opinions and two cents on what you should do as if they are so involved in your decision making they should contribute to the outcome. As they say, if you want to tell me what to do in my house, you best be ready to pay rent. You would have to give me something to listen to you and take notes!

In case, people do NOT know, I am full-grown over here, and I won't have anyone telling me what to do in my house, and they are not putting nothing on the table. Do you catch my drift? If I fail or mess up, it is at my OWN dime and time - you feel me?

Let me say it another way. Consider any goal or dream you set to achieve for yourself. If you say you want to buy a house by a certain time, for example. You say I saved up ten thousand, but you know you need twenty thousand to buy what you want.

If you are still willing to bend for everyone else, you will try to justify buying something else, or even

Don't Let Your Dreams Go!

buying the house years from now. People will always have problems, and their problems don't have to be yours. You remember what I said, let it go!

If you have people living in your house, it is time to have each of them pay you something so you can use that money to achieve some of the things you want. As parents, our children can think they deserve to keep living off of our hard work, and cancel or delay your plans. We will always be a parent, but that doesn't mean I have to consistently sacrifice what I want for grown children to be happy.

I am no longer your bodyguard and it is not my job to make you happy. I laugh when people tell me their grown children are staying with them and paying no rent. I simply reply back to them, "Why not?" They look at me puzzled and dazed like they see a fly or bee going around the room. My face doesn't hide my strong disagreement because I don't see what the excuse could be.

I understand some children can come back home and spend a few weeks or months tops, trying to get back on their feet after college, a divorce, or some major life change. No problem, what I don't understand is why you would make your life twice as hard because your children refuse to grow up. I have three grown daughters with their own sets of challenges.

They all have degrees, and it wouldn't be possible for them not because that was the rule of my house. You had to have at least a bachelors to stay here. When you set rules like that, your children will have to respect you or get out. There is no negotiating, in this house is not a democracy - I am NOT asking, I am telling.

I was not apologetic about what me and Glenn decided about education and preparing our daughters for life. It is not our job as parents to coddle our children and keep them from growing up. We have to let them live and grow up so we can dream again if we had to delay our plans.

I am not like others and I never put Melvina on the shelf. I know some things I had to do differently than I would have without children, but my life is about right now, no matter the circumstances. You, however, have to be honest and say did I get what I wanted out of life?

Did I become all I had hoped to become, or is my life falling short because I am taking on problems that are not mine? When my children finished college and flew the nest, they all knew they couldn't come back here. They know they have to make it out there and they pushed themselves to be able to do it. Them all having degrees and the ability to fend for themselves was a requirement to prepare them for life because hard times will come. When something hard comes they cannot run to me and dump their problems on me and expect me to fix them.

Some of us have lost our dreams because we are too busy saving everyone else. Sometimes, you have to move back and allow people to drown. Allow them to fail, I mean. We learn the best when we fail, I failed, and look at me. When I started as a medical coder, my first few jobs were not the greatest experience for me. I failed forward, I learned from my mistakes, I learned to spend more time on what I didn't know, and sought more education to better my skills so I could demand the type of money I wanted to make.

    I make no apologies for being who I am and what I have grown to become, because there is still a whole lot mo' to Melvina. This happy challenge I have to balance my life is what keeps me moving toward my dreams. If you are stagnated, you need to find yourself and what you feel is your purpose in life. We are all here to accomplish some things, and as our children grow older, we can redefine what our goals are too. Mine have shifted a lot.

    I used to work hard and look forward to coming home, or already being home, and seeing my children and husband. Now, they are all grown and living their lives. My focus is on my husband and I. As our family grows, it is my prayer to be close to my daughters, their spouses, and my grandchildren; but none of that is here now. I have to find out what is good for Melvina now. Some things don't change, Love, Family, and Money. These are my pillars and have been my focus, but my why behind these three things does shift as I keep on living.

    I re-evaluate what I want in my life all the time and my biggest piece of advice, you need to assess what you want in your life. If you want to buy a house that requires twenty thousand dollars and you got ten, if someone asks you to do stuff or loan them anything, you say "No, not at this time." If you want to be bold, you can say it like this, "No, that doesn't line up with my goals. I am not going to do this for you now or in the future. I pray the best for you." Then leave it alone. People keep bringing you their problems because they think you are "Mrs. Fix It." Again, what did I say…Let It Go!!

It is time to exercise your power by using the word "no." If they quit their job and they are broke, it looks like there will be rough times ahead for them. That wasn't your decision, so why are you paying for it? Stop allowing people to eat off your dime and live off of you when they are not willing to contribute anything. If they are, but them coming around is something you don't want, don't be afraid to say, "no" still. The main question is are you scared? Is "NO" in your vocabulary?

When you are afraid to say "no," you are compromising your dream. You are funding other people's dreams instead of your own. You are allowing your feelings, emotions, and other people to come before your dreams. I want to tell you, don't compromise or do something for others that costs you your dreams. It is NOT worth it, life is too short!!

You might think it is the right thing to do, to put everyone else's needs before yours. You might consider this a good sacrifice, but what has been the payoff? Has putting money into other people's dreams helped you to be more fulfilled? Has it put you in a better position to put you first or for others to help you achieve your goals? Has your sacrifice led to others caring for you or made you the Santa Claus of your family?

Don't Let Your Dreams Go!

There is nothing wrong with focusing on your dreams and goals more. This is how I operate, and I am not afraid to win come hell or high water. I will let people go, negativity, and any unfair judgment in a heartbeat. You don't have to hold on to other people's negativity and foolishness. Keep your dream ahead of you and do not change course no matter what because you are the one who will be the greatest impacted by your choices.

So, build the life you want to live. Yes, be selfish. I call a spade a spade, which is exactly what it is. I choose me, Melvina first because Melvina rises up. When all people over here rise up - advance in education, traveling, owning their houses, generational wealth, and the best health care- this list goes on, they will be on my level. I like the air up here; it feels great, and I am not coming down. I am still telling you when I say Let It Go, I mean Let It Go!!

Remember that you are a woman. Before you became a wife, a mother, an employee, etc, you were a woman with a dream. You are now choosing to add things to your life, no problem. The problem becomes, why did you allow these things to cloud your dreams?

Why did you allow these choices to make you feel you can no longer achieve your dreams?

The truth, the proof is in the pudding and you can make it happen. You can be a woman who has it all. You can be married, raise wonderful children, and be fulfilled personally. You can achieve your dreams and be in the club that is happy with their lives. I know, many are two peas in the pod with those who have abandoned their dreams and these people don't mind being vocal about how marriage and children have changed their goals in life.

Please mute people who are not adding value and helping you achieve what you need out of life. Your dreams are part of why you are here. We all have things we said when we were a little girl that we wanted to do, why have you abandoned that girl? Why do you feel that life has a right to keep stealing away what you promised her? Will she ever have a say or be important in your life again?

Please tell me you are with me. YOU have to get authority over your dreams. YOU have to remember that living your dreams means you have to work for it! You might have to work longer nights. YOU may have to go back to school while you take care of your children and husband.

YOU may need to talk to hubby about your sexual needs and changes that may need to occur so you can get things done for you too. It is not easy to achieve your goals with family, but it needs to be done. YOU feel me, the operative word with this is YOU.

Don't Let Your Dreams Go!

You don't want to be a woman who is growing bitter because she feels not seen or heard. We can suffer internally for how our life is set up and miss the root cause. The truth, we all need self-fulfillment. That doesn't come solely from making everyone else happy, but you too. You have to stop discrediting what you want out of life and feeling bad that you want something for yourself.

You go to everyone's games, cook the meals, decorate the parties, and show up for others, but you will have to ask people to do that for you too! You have to work to achieve your dreams too! You have to practice asking them to be flexible with their schedules like you are for theirs. Don't be afraid to speak up for yourself and for what you want out of life. You are not just the person to make everyone else happy and become miserable. This is your life too!

I am NOT gonna lie to you, I cannot be Susie Homemaker and CEO. I am not focusing on how to fit other people's roles, I am putting my heart into how I can make things happen that we need as a family, but still achieve my goals. I don't cook and clean. I can cook, but I don't. I don't clean my house, I work hard and pay someone to do it for me.

I work hard, and I love who I am. I see the value in who God made me to be and how He is steering my life through my choices. I am blessed and I know it. I don't apologize for that and anyone in my life is going to work to have me in it like I do. I don't think a man you marry should have access to you unless he works for it. I don't think any woman should let a man pull her panties down and stick it to her, and he didn't put any work in to get there.

Yes, and I said what I said. Trust me, with only five sex partners in my entire life - when my panties drop, it will be because HE put in some work for a few months. I don't look at the ding-dong and be like I gotta have it. Instead, they look at me and say they got to work for ME. I know my worth!

I know stepping on some toes, but, "no" I wasn't letting no one touch me without putting in the work to get that close to me. Even with my friends and family. I do have standards for what I expect and how people will treat me. I don't let anyone treat me any old kind of way. I am valuable, I love me, and I won't have people in my space just sucking up air. They will work like I do to stay around me or they will leave. You gotta keep your dreams at the forefront by remembering you are valuable.

One of my quotes to live by is in a song, called Jireh by Maverick City….

> I'm already loved
> I'm already chosen
> I know who I am
> I know what you've spoken
> I'm already loved
> More than I could even imagine
> And that is enough

I am not saying that it will be a happy ending for everybody when I am going for my dreams. Some people are going to have to feel some kind of way while they let me work on my dreams. I know that I want to help everybody, but not everyone will agree with my operation. Not everyone will appreciate how I move. This is when you have to be prepared to say "Oh, well!"

This is my stance, I am unapologetically me. I am who I say I am and I use my authority to mean what I say. I have things I want to accomplish and you have to have that mindset. Life will go on and you cannot ball up when your dreams cause others discomfort. You have to allow this process to become really simple. You are not selfish because you want to take care of yourself, that makes you mindful.

No one wants to be a slave, or at least I don't. I want to own my life, my decisions, my choices for what I will have and what I will and won't do. Some people won't like my choices, hell, some people won't like me. I can deal with that. But can you? Can you deal with people not liking your choices? If you can't, why not? Those same people are okay with you not being happy or getting what you want, so why must you be a loser for their happiness?

If things can come to the middle, great, but I am not here to make everyone happy. I am here to accomplish what Melvina was put on earth to do, come hell or high water. You have to get to a point where you can love yourself like how you love everyone else. To hell with people's discomfort, let them squirm to see you happy, and one day they will get it. And if not, don't worry about it. Sleep peacefully at night if you know you are doing the right thing by yourself and others.

Melvina W.

Don't be afraid to communicate what you need and what you want. I choose to be clear about what I am looking for and define what choosing me first means. To choose you first doesn't mean you are a selfish person, BUT it does mean you exercise a selfish stance and choose YOU first before others.

For sure it means you know what you want out of life. You are picky about who is in your space. You know the team you are building to accomplish what you want out of life. Don't just accept anything someone wants to give you.

Tell people, jobs, or situations, this is not good enough if it isn't. Remember without you there is NO happiness, no good quality of life, no living, etc. Remember, to throw some funk on it and be selfish to ask for what you want but just DON'T be a selfish person.

I had to walk away from relationships, jobs, and people that were not putting down what I was looking for. I said, "No, thank you," and never looked back. If you feel guilty about accomplishing good things for yourself and those you love, I want to encourage you to let the guilt go. Let it go. To accomplish generational wealth, you will have to tell others no. You have to be willing to let go of the people holding you back from things that you want; this is good for you and them.

I have heard some stories of how women are putting their whole life policy money on their children getting things. They are putting all their money on their children's shoes, their trips, and stuff they need. They tell me, "They have to give it all up." Where does this

Don't Let Your Dreams Go!

mentality come from that says you have to give up your ambitions and career for family?

I take myself on trips and when my husband and I had younger children, that didn't stop us from getting away. And that didn't stop us from taking the entire family as well on trips. We need to stop complaining about how we had to put money on this and that.

You said the money couldn't be spent on yourself five and ten years ago. More time has gone by, and you still talking about, "I had to put" my money or time on something else OTHER than yourself. So, when are you going to remember yourself and put yourself first in this situation? Again…Let It Go!!

Stop believing that you are stuck. Stop feeling guilty about the things you want and don't allow others to shut doors you want to be open. I like options, so I make choices to keep my options open. I choose to determine what my happiness will be and I control if I will be happy or sad. Stop giving your power to other people.

I remember this person told me she had to step up and take care of her mom because my other siblings said no. I asked her, "Why?" She said because the others said no. They had larger houses, bigger bank accounts, and more to share. "So, why are you struggling to say no?" I have parents too, and if I say my parents aren't staying with me, then they won't. Not to say I won't make sure they are good, but I won't let anyone make me do something I don't want to.

Melvina W.

If your siblings can say no, why can't you? And before you even say, "Well, I don't want to be that person, like them?" What person is that I am asking? They, your family, just said no, they dropped the ball and you over there picking it up saying yes! They are going on with their life, going on trips, making more money than you, going out on dates, and all that. While you are still making sacrifices, spending your money on that loved one, talking about someone had to take care of them.

So, what is that you again? You love them just that much? Okay, who loves you that much? Who will reciprocate that feelings and do all of this for you one day?

Why do you allow others to force you to do what you don't want and at times, can't do? I remember a job I had that would bring me to tears. It made me feel like a slave while on that job. I got that check, and as I wiped my tears, I said this is a good day to quit. I can do better, and I have been. As you turn the pages with me, I am going to drill in your heart to let it the fuck go. Because life is too short and you have no other option if you hope to have what you want out of life.

My happiness comes first. I had to make it that way because when we are focused on making everyone else happy, it doesn't work. You will get drained and people won't appreciate it or you; which will become a major problem. Let people go who are mooching off of me and expecting me to put down my happiness for theirs. YOU need to be happy and shine your light so brightly that they might be impacted by your joy.

Don't Let Your Dreams Go!

When people see you, they buy into what you are selling by seeing if it first makes you happy. I think this is what so many people get wrong. We try to sell others on how wonderful something or somebody is, but they are looking at if you are happy or not to make their choice. We cannot hide our happiness or if we are not that long. If you are hiding it, why? You are just getting older. Your body, face, etc will fade over time. So the sooner you are honest about your own happiness the better.

It is your turn. You have been waiting and now it is your turn. If you are asking when will it be my turn? I am gonna answer that for you, right now. Your turn is NOW, you are NOT dead yet-- so your turn is NOW. It is always my turn because I am making things happen. This is the game I am playing to win and you have to get that mindset too. When you show up, you are prepared and ready to go because you know it is your turn!

Are you committed to living your dreams? Are you ready to move things forward? Do you think you have waited long enough? Well if not, I do! Hell, it is my turn because I am putting in the work to make myself happy. I don't look to others to do what I should do for myself. You have to take accountability for your own dreams happening and your happiness. If you don't like where you are at in life, change it!

I too have been consumed as a mother and wife. It was hard and difficult so I know where you are or where you are working from. In my late twenties and early thirties when I launched my business, I felt that my dreams were just too hard to obtain. I was losing focus because the bills were coming in, and things were getting turned on and off. I was losing focus for five or ten minutes when I questioned what I was building, but I chose not to meditate on that thought for too long. I do NOT stall there when things are bleak and I am down like four flat tires. I do NOT stall there!

I can have these downward moments, but I do not let them reshape my dreams. I start making choices. Children went to bed early, I didn't have sex that night, there was no shower, there was no talking on the phone, no shopping, no spending any extra money; the list goes on. I was focused, driven, and motivated on the changes I needed to make.

I had to stop having these thoughts and not allow my feelings or emotions to erase what I was wanting to make happen. Don't allow your down moments to define your dreams or erase them entirely. Don't delay your dreams for years at a time because you might not feel it at the moment. You can do this and I am a reminder! The proof is in the pudding!! So, where is your pudding - you better start right NOW getting the proof!!

My dreams have changed over time, no doubt. I didn't know what business I wanted to have, but I had a dream to have one. I knew I wanted to own my house and pay it off early in life. That happened. For me, I don't think it is that my dreams change, but they evolve and get bigger.

I don't stop, I will NOT stop, I am all about

Don't Let Your Dreams Go!

moving forward. When I started Infinity HIM Medical Coding School, my goal was to see how else I could be of benefit. I began mentoring, offering job placement, and helping to secure my medical coders' futures after coding class.

Then, I went on to start numerous businesses. They are not my bread and butter, but they are part of my dream. Not everything you do has to be important to everyone else or even make sense. I like my book collection because it makes me happy. I don't have to explain this to anyone and if my books sold a few copies, I would be happy because I did this for Melvina.

I am happy to say I have a podcast that is on iHeart, Spotify, Apple Podcast, and ten other stations. I didn't have that in my plan, but my dream got bigger! Your dream can get bigger too. I had plans to have four children, but ended up with three, but then I got a bonus daughter while on a vacation to Kenya. Glenn and I didn't plan for more children, but I got someone added to my dream and she is a blessing to our lives.

Melvina W.

your dreams to grow, but don't lose sight of the goal ever. Don't erase what is important to you to do something more beneficial for someone else to your own detriment. You have to be part of your future, an active part, or life will keep going on and you will be the miserable one. You will be sitting there with excuses and wondering could'da, would'da, should'da. Time will keep moving ahead - NOT backward!!

Whatever you need to do, to make your life goals happen, do it. My dream didn't include going back to school for my Masters with three small children. I had four-year-old twin girls and a six-year-old when I went back to school and graduated. I launched my business in 2013. I am telling you it has taken years to get a lot of what I can say I have today. I am more than fifty years old.

So, I am telling YOU to spend the money on your education and be prepared to put in the work to make the money and achieve your goals. But please don't spend all your money on a sucky major such as History, English, Business Administration, etc exclusively. If you do not personally know Tyler Perry, then you might want to rethink Theater and Acting as a major solely. Let that be a backup while you become an Engineer or Computer major.

Pick something that a robot will not be doing in the next 6 months or something that is in high demand to get you employment when you graduate from college. I didn't say it was easy and I know it is getting harder to do, BUT I know it can be done. Again, the proof is in the pudding. What is in your pudding?

Don't Let Your Dreams Go!

You have to pay for your education, and if Trump has his way, there will be no financial aid or free money to go. If you are spending your dollars and cents, you better make education count from now on. Pick majors that can help you financially build wealth and provide for your family. My life started as a computer programmer. I quickly shifted gears to the medical field, and soon after became a medical coder after going back to school. It wasn't a straight line, but I rolled with the changes and I became all the wiser.

One of the best things I have learned about my students that really touches my heart is seeing how they change to believing they can. I had a student who came to me and told me how she is now single, no man, and her children are off on their own. She stopped worrying about everyone else, to focus on her education and goals, to have something for herself.

This is how you reinvent yourself. YOU have to have an abundance mindset, believe, and know you are enough. YOU have to have the audacity to believe you can and do the work.

I am here to push you along as you let it go. Let's keep moving on.

What The Hell Happened

You got to want this. You have to want something for yourself because if you don't, no one else can do it for you. I can talk till I am blue in the face, but that won't change a thing for you in your life. I want you to understand I might sound strong or direct to you now, but it has taken me time to build and clearly understand the assignment.

I had to learn to prioritize my life like any woman, wife, or mother does. We don't always come first, but after seeing where that got me, I learned I could not survive like that. At twenty-two years old, I knew I wanted to buy a house. When I made that happen, I knew the next thing was possible because I was tracking my progress. You have to make good and solid decisions consistently, or you can burn down what you are building and lose your momentum.

I want to keep you encouraged, but you know I have to do it my way. I have to ask, does your life include what you want? I know in the last chapter, I tried reminding you about the younger version of yourself. So what the hell happened? Why don't you have what you said you would by this time in your life? I am listening.

If we don't talk about the things holding us back and find solutions, we will never get ahead. I want us to dive deeper into what happened so we know how to get out of the mud. We cannot stay buried in the sand and expect life to take care of us. We have to guide and direct the ship. The direction you are heading in is up to you, and I want to ask, where in the hell are you going?

If you don't know, I don't know what else I can say. When people sign up for my medical coding school, in orientation, I ask them, "So what do you want from this program?" followed by, "What are you trying to accomplish in life?" Based on their answers to these two questions, I can sum up who will finish the program and how well they can do if they remain focused.

I don't have a crystal ball to see the future, but I know if you can see a vision ahead, you are more likely to reach your goals than people who are spiraling on what-if scenarios. I never wanted to be a person with excuses. When people started saying I would have been in school sooner if I didn't have to do this. Or if this wouldn't have happened, I would have done that. I tell them, "Well, you are not dead yet. What is your excuse now?"

We have to have a sense of urgency when we do anything. When we think, we have until forever, we don't take life as seriously as we should. We can be guilty of delaying our dreams for years because we didn't see a purpose in moving on them now. We were blinded by distractions and could not see what the future held for us. The sad truth, you never will if you don't start prioritizing what you must do now to get there.

Should'da, would'da, could'da scenarios don't work as I said earlier? Don't sit there and say, that's her; everybody just doesn't have it. Why you don't and why you can't obtain it. What makes me so different? Don't we all put our pants on one leg at a time?

I am 400 pounds, black, and half deaf. So it's not that you can't but it's will you? If you will not, I am doing 100 miles on the highway, if you are going the speed limit, move out of my way! Wake up. People are out here going for what they want. They are charging ahead to create their own story, so why not you? Give me something to work with!

If you want nothing out of life, we will not be friends. You can keep this book and it will help you when you want something. I want to be clear: I have nothing for you if you want nothing; there is nothing I can do. I mean it when I say give me something to work with!

Do you need some hypothetical, would'da, could'da, should'da fluff and buff? Nawww, that is NOT me, my mind is made up, so I look for people who are ready to win. Look at this. I help people get a plan to get into medical coding when they are serious.

Melvina W.

I have various limits to get you started, but if you have excuses, all of them are expensive. But let me tell you, they are $25, $50, $75, $150, $450, and $900. You can get the education you need to get a job that pays 50k a year for under 1k; tell me, what am I missing?

Nothing. The truth is that most people have excuses for why their lives went off the railings, and those same excuses keep them stuck year after year. It used to break my heart to see people struggling when they didn't have to. Now, it doesn't bother me because I realized a long time ago some people would choose to be broke while others work to win. I work to win, and I believe you want to, also.

I want to be around like-minded people no matter where you are starting from or you might be right now. I am here to help you within my reason to come up higher. So let's roll. I have a driver do most of my driving, but today I am going to take you around the landmines that have been blowing shit up in yo' life. If stuff is flying everywhere and you can't see your way out, listen up. I am about to give you some answers you need to hear.

What The Hell Happened

The first thing you need to turn to and look at is what you are fitting into your life. If you are "broke as a joke", you don't have any time to socialize. You need to be focused on grinding to get your family out of the hole they are in. I bet NOT see a new purse, a girl's trip, or any other plans that mean money is going out on anything. If you smoke, put it down, quit, any drug habits, gotta go.

I personally don't do drugs or smoke, but if you are broke, these are luxuries you cannot afford. Having these habits costs money, and they are not meant for broke people, but they make a lot of people penniless. I had a family member who struggled to get their life together because one step forward was a few back. It broke my heart, but at the same time, I wasn't going to fund his habit. Stop helping people who will use your money for stupid stuff that is not helping them. Let them suffer if they must.

You can make time later to have fun, but right now, you need a new job and maybe a second job. You cannot afford to shop or hang out, so take that out of your mind. Don't think you are owed something; you are not. Your infrastructure is not set, and you have not done anything worth celebrating. I am not the person who thinks everyone on the team needs a trophy. If you lost, embrace the loss and do better. It is not the end of the world, but celebrating failure I have a problem with. I said what I said.

Now, I am not saying don't do anything to have fun, boycott sex–hell no. But I am saying you need to prioritize getting out of the hole. When I had to burrow down and get two jobs to pay off debts from a house and get our family in a good financial position, I did it. We both had to endure those tough times, but now that we are out, we can do better with personal time and not work weekends, etc.

When the infrastructure is there, you can add more things to your life that are fun. But don't get into the Amazon honey phase where you buy yourself something to feel better about yourself. Focus on doing better to earn something for yourself. We have to get back to understanding the value of earning improvements and not being given them. Learning to work is a virtue and a necessity if you want more out of life.

Let's say you are out of the weeds, your life is good, you just want more. Cool, cool. I am a wife, a mother, a business owner, an author, and a podcaster. I choose how I will spend my time. I am deciding where I want it to be spent and how much. You don't have to give everyone else every part of your day and leave nothing for yourself. Make time for your goals and spend time alone to reflect on what you want now. Things change, and so can you.

Don't think all your money and time is being stored up for everyone else. Take the trip you want. If your friends can't go, still go! I don't think we should sit at home or miss out on what we want to do because others can't go. I like first class, and I do the damn thing. I am not worried about who goes or not. I am doing this for me and when you work hard, celebrate yourself.

What The Hell Happened

For some of you, you don't know how to take a break! You need to get out, have sex, enjoy your husband, spend a family trip away from the house, and bond. Don't spend every day and hour working or slaving away to save money you don't get to enjoy. Keep your marriage and children close. Don't neglect them, but give everyone a piece of you, and you will be fine.

You can have it all, love, peace, money, husband, and children. Again, the proof is in the pudding; what is in your pudding? Let me take it a step further if your pudding doesn't have any proof. YOU need to Let It Go, whatever that IT is ... period!

I am not saying it will be easy, or there won't be any problems, but they will work themselves out. I will talk a bit more about me but right now, we are talking about you. Don't feel guilty about missing out on time with friends or family if you can't do something. Use your calendar and build it out. Plan what you want to do, but don't overextend yourself. Let people know you will do it when you can, but know what you are working with.

One thing about time that I have learned and you do if you don't know. You can't get time back. Once it is wasted, or whatever, it is gone. You can apologize for your actions, but you are not taking nothing back. You cannot go backward; you only go forward. So keep your focus and attention on that.

Too often, people want to drag you backward with negative thinking, bringing up the past, and bitchin or whining about it–but that doesn't change anything.

Melvina W.

You cannot change the past. But hear me, I am not saying you cannot address stuff in your past, but don't stay there. You have to move forward. Dealing with the past can be uncomfortable, this I know.

So, what am I saying? If you sit there and dwell on the past for years, you are going to be stuck. What the hell are we talking about, if the people you bring up are not in your future? What mistakes did you make? Okay, learn from them. But why are you beating yourself up or allowing others to do that to you when they are a non-issue that is just stopping your progress.

Ground that is lost is lost. If you steal from a man, you can make that right by repaying what was taken. If you have offended someone, you can apologize for it. You cannot pull back your actions but you can make good on it. So go out and do great so you can rebuild. Commit to rebuilding instead of going back over the past. But move forward.

If you sit there and do nothing, you will become nothing and have nothing. If you allow people to dump the past on you, their problems, or things that weigh you down, it is up to you to change that behavior. If you keep living a cycle of repetition, that would be your choice–it's a dumb one, but it's your choice. You need to know that you are enough and you don't have to pick up the pieces and fix other people's problems.

But I can tell you this, if you don't change, you will look up again and say, "What the Hell is Still happening in my life?" You don't want to stay a follower all your life at some point, you have to become a leader of yourself. It is okay to listen to other people's opinions but you don't have to agree. Stop agreeing to get along, but think for yourself. If what you have been doing is a problem, make a choice to change.

One thing about Melvina, if someone tells me they don't see anything wrong with their lives, I let it go. You need to let it go. We are not superheroes with capes flying around to solve people's crises. There are some people we both know that will never get their shit together if we keep bailing them out. So stop it. Keep your mind and protect your time. I am giving you the real, but do what you will.

Everyone needs to be accountable. So whatever the plan is, you need to make sure everyone sticks to it. You have to make sure that everyone is on point. As a family, you set the tone. What you allow is what others will expect. I know, as a mother, it can hurt when our children reject us or get slick in the mouth. But I want to tell you, a guilt trip won't get you anywhere.

You need to bury that deep and let it go. You need to put your foot down and expect that people will respect it, and if they don't, make them. You might say, "Well, Melvina. How am I supposed to do that? Nobody listens to me." My response, "Because you don't make them. What happens if someone doesn't do what you tell them to do?"

If the short answer is nothing, you won't kick them out, take anything, or you set rules that you will NOT keep, they are going to run all over you and make you a creampuff. They are going to treat you like a

Melvina W.

friend, or a minion they tell what to do. But you have all the responsibility. You are the one paying the bills out here looking like "Boo Boo The Fool" letting your children tell you what to do!

You better let their guilt trip go. They don't care about your feelings if they are doing that and neither should you care about theirs. The world doesn't care about your feelings but rules and protocol. If you break the law, you are going to pay for that. If you steal, you will get the penalty. There are no passes in life that are guaranteed. I know some people might not like what I am about to say, but if you got something through stealing, and someone asks for their stuff back, are you the wrong person to make them pay? Even if it has been several years in the making?

There are people out here arguing about stuff that belongs to other people. If you stole something, no matter how long ago, and they find you and want it back, you owe them and should pay it. That is a simple principle that I think we make complicated because our feelings get involved.

If you want your house to flow, you have to pull your emotions out of it and look at the facts, then decide if you want to do mercy and stuff like that. Do that sparingly because too much mercy leads to disrespect. They won't appreciate it and you will be back to where you started. Catch my drift, you feel me?

The next thing is to clean up your house. If it is time to move people out or tell people no. Why should you be uncomfortable in your own home? Where you pay bills, you should be happy. You should not have to put up with other people's nonsense. You should be determined to be happy in your home, and you should not feel obligated to deal with others you don't like just because others are going through their own stuff.

Stop suffering because other people are down on their luck. If I have a family member knock on my door who has not cleared the Melvina's test to be here, they are not invited. They would be lucky to reach my doorstep. Some may say I am mean. I don't give a Sugar-Honey-Iced-Tea. I am not going to be uncomfortable in my own space. I don't recommend others should be either. If you don't like me, and I don't like you, it can be that way. If you knock on the door, you should know already my answer is no, you cannot stay here.

Put them out if they don't respect you. If you don't like them, and they don't like you, save your time and energy and say "no." I don't have the impression that the word "no" is ever wrong to say. I heard that there are people who feel bad about saying "no." I don't understand how those people can think saying no is wrong.

If you believe this, there is something fundamentally wrong here. You are not in my circle and we are not in the same space. You cannot go where I shop, or stand where I stand if you cannot rise up and say yes or no to something. We have a problem–actually you have a problem.

Anyone who cannot say "no" will have a hard time even being able to stand on a solid yes. These people are fickle, and you shouldn't trust them because they will go with the flow, and they lack conviction, power, courage and all. Nobody wants to deal with a cream puff or marshmallow type person who can't think for themselves. At least I don't, and I made doggone sure I raised daughters who are clearly NOT like that. Some of this advice bites me in the butt, but I would rather they had their own minds and opinions than for them to be "yes people."

You hurt yourself if you can't tell others no or you feel it is wrong to think about what is best for you. You will lose every time, and you need to throw this kind of thinking into the trash right now to stay afloat through the next few chapters of this book. If you don't agree, I want you to challenge yourself to think like me a little bit longer. Try saying no and see what happens. When you say no, you will move things out of your life. You can stop things from happening anymore when you exercise your right to say no. You are cleaning up your house when you set boundaries using the word no.

I know it is not easy to start moving our grip off of people's lives because saying no could also mean seeing others grow. When you tell your children "no," you cannot stay here anymore because it is time for them to grow and explore life on their own, you're helping. I knew when my daughters had to go away to college, they needed to leave my house to live in a dorm.

Yes, they still needed my money and were on my dime, but they started to explore their own freedom. When we rob our children of this needed growth, we rob ourselves of saying yes to the things we want to do. I made it clear early on that they will need to find their own house and start taking responsibility for their lives.

They knew that no sucky degree was going to provide shelter, food, and the resources they would need to take care of themselves. I am not trying to have a forty-year-old child living with me because they are chasing their dreams. I want to chase mine, too, so it only makes sense to help them grow up. You only rob yourself when you allow your children to outstay their welcome in your house.

If you did the right thing raising your children to help them understand money and how to manage bills, then it is time to send them on their way. If they have a mindset that they know more than you, they can move on earlier. I would say when they finish college, it's time to go because what would be the purpose of becoming grown if you are going to live off of me always? No grown child 30 or 40 years old should still be suckling your mother's titty.

This is not a cultural thing. I know some people will say in my family or my culture this is what we do. Again, I understand staying home while you build but don't waste my time. Some children aren't building anything but enjoying subsidized living. You are robbing them of adulthood. They need to grow the hell up, or you need to shut up when they are popping babies out on your dime because you didn't teach em' to have their own.

If you are guilty of this, good news, it can

change. Yes, for some of you softies, it will be hard– but mark my words it is necessary. You will be taking care of them all of their lives if you don't put your foot down and let them put on their grown man or woman draws. Trust me when I say this: you are going to be the one stressing out, not them.

If your children live with you, there is a disconnect, and somebody failed to understand the assignment. There are one of two issues: either you messed up and need help to live on your own, or they messed up and don't know how to live on their own. Or you both have a flaw, and need each other to live. It is hardly ever a mutual decision but often out of obligation or necessity. I think that is where you messed up.

Money gives you options, and if you don't have it, you can be forced to do stuff you don't want to do. You might not like this, but if you want my opinion, I think it is embarrassing, shameful, and disgraceful to rob people of their freedom to live how they want to. When people are selfish enough not to consider others, it is one of the worst kinds of disrespect. Some people don't have any plans of getting their own but want to live off people like leeches or parasites. It's wrong, and I said what I said.

I know other countries and third-world countries may need the help of each other. I am not talking about them. In this country, you have the ability to make a path that works. You can earn the money, you can take the responsibility, you can build the life you want. I am not talking about people who are building. I am talking about those who are happy staying with their momma.

What The Hell Happened

They buy cars, do drugs, blow their money on clothes, and doing things that don't matter. You see them waste money, and you give them excuses or think because they have a few hundred dollars on the rent they are fine.

If you didn't stay with your parents, why is it okay they can do that to you? Do you feel they will fail? Have you not trained them? If you have, then what's the problem? You need to let it go! Whatever they say, they are trying to guilt trip you into letting them stay. Stop it. They need to move on and live their lives so you can enjoy yours. The baby phase is over, and they need to grow up and provide for themselves because that is what we do.

I have always believed in family, so I am not knocking you being close to your children. When I went on vacation, I took everybody. I made moments for us all to share and was a parent to them, a mother I still am. However, I will give them what they need to be decent women in this society. My goal is to see them take care of themselves, to be wives, have children, and raise their families.

It was never an option for them to build a family in my house. I am the only full-grown woman in my house. I was never their friend. My goal is for them all to respect me and think of me as their mother and not as their provider. I am training them to provide for themselves. I have a lot of friends who will state that their children cannot make it because life is too expensive.

That is an excuse in my opinion. I have three

Melvina W.

daughters out there taking care of themselves. Some tell me they leave when they are married, but they are single, and they aren't living with their parents. So why are they holding on to their grown children? Why won't the grown children move out? They only sit there and say they have no money but what choices have they been making on why they have nothing set up?

My thoughts on my parenting style is that I did a hell of a GOOD job! I am living free, calling a spade a spade. If you have a style of parenting that doesn't permit your children to live life but stay stuck holding their skirts, there is a problem with the teaching style. Children are not babies forever, and they must grow up! You are failing your children by allowing them to stay. They are running from responsibility, and one day, when you are dead and gone, they will be lost and forced to do what you should have: Kick them out of the nest!

Birds got it right. They understand nature better than any of us. No emotions are involved, although I am sure they love their babies too. They force them to fly because a walking bird is a dead bird. Parents need to prepare their children for life and death, circumstances and problems, and choices and outcomes. The way you allow them to live will shape the adult they become and, ultimately, the type of spouse and parent also.

So, if you want to change their ways or yours, encourage them to get an education. Tell them they have to get an education or certifications. Don't allow guilt to shut you down or distract you from doing what you must. You have to let them go.

What The Hell Happened

But you might not do this because you feel it is too late. You might feel guilty about putting them out, but grow a pair of balls and put them out. You might say I don't have a degree, so how can I make them get a degree? You want them to do better than you, right? You started late, but better late than never. Be a better parent now than before. Don't be their friend, be their parent.

Children need discipline and boundaries, period. You will offend their feelings. So what. They will get over it and learn to respect it. My children didn't like everything I said and did, but they respected it. It was my house, my rules, and my dime. So yes, it went my way. I am not apologizing for things going the way I want them to go and for those who didn't like it. I will own up to my faults, though. I have a heart and love my children, but I made it clear, "We are not friends."

I do not wear my heart on my sleeve because I know better. I get hurt like everyone else, but I refuse to stay there. You have places to go to and things to do. So don't allow yourself to wallow in hurt. Let it go! It is three words, and it is really simple. Some people are just negative and want to inflict pain and bring no resolution. These relationships are salty and need work.

If you both are living, it is not too late to get things going in the right direction if you missed the first boat. My knees are not built for bending like that, and I am not going to waste my time praying about something that hard. If I have to let something go, I do. I give people as much space as they need, and I take the same liberty.

Melvina W.

Time is not your friend if you are late in the game and you have a salty relationship with your children. You need to use your voice, use common sense, and speak to them with it. If they don't want to use it and think everything you say is wrong, they are never going to get it, but you can. They have time as they breathe, but when you die, or they die, it is too late. So try not to wait that long and nip this chaos in the butt, I'm telling you.

I made this conversation a whole chapter because I have seen this so much, and it bothers me. Not that I believe I have it right, if you like what you do, carry on if that works for you. But if it doesn't. You are sad, broke, lonely, and looking at what the hell happened. You need to start with growing a strong voice. Standing on what you want. Kicking people out or holding them accountable.

I am not saying you cannot welcome your children home who need help for six months here and there. This is for people who intend to live off of you for years to come and many until you die. Then they want to pick up in your place and never create their own. They don't know what to do with what you leave them with because they have never been responsible. Don't waste your wealth on children you can't trust now.

Your legacy is yours. You cannot control how your children live but you can control how you will be remembered when you leave here. Don't waste your legacy on children or people who don't appreciate your efforts and what you give. Give it to someone else, hell an organization can help you put it to work. But don't leave your money to no got doggone cat or something. I don't understand that at all, but whatever. That's your money, too. Do what you want and carry on.

Try to focus on keeping your heart pure because you control what makes or breaks you. You cannot worry too long about others because your power is not in their choices but yours. Let me tell you what I wish:

- I wish I did not have to travel for medical coding to get the infrastructure built that I have today…
- I wish that people would accept me for me
- I wish that people would acknowledge me for the person I am to them or was to them
- I wish people would communicate properly with me
- I wish family members would walk an inch in my shoes and just try to comprehend or understand where I am coming from and where I have been
- I wish I could feel more loved from some of my family members
- I wish I could guarantee that we have enough time to mend any broken hearts in my family
- I wish some family members could LET GO of the freaking past and move forward…
- I wish people would stop hiding behind their same ole' past and HEAL
- I wish people would stop hiding behind words and making assumptions about other people's circumstances
- I wish I didn't even have to go down this road of, I wish, if I could of, would of, should of….

Melvina W.

- I wish people could see the forest beyond the trees
- I wish people would just be real about the situation instead of dancing around
- I wish people to be more real about themselves
- I wish people would call a spade a spade - it is what it is
- I wish people loved each other more, at least like
- I wish it was compassion and respect for all
- I wish grown children one day will have a complete understanding of what parenthood looks like
- I wish grown children get off of their mommy's titties and grown up (out of their parents' house)
- I wish to have even more generational wealth, and hopefully, you do too
- I wish I could stop….
- AND HERE IS THE KICKER, someone in HELL wish they could have ice-cold water, BUT THAT doesn't mean you are gonna get it!!
- So, with that being stated - this is WHY I say LET IT GO…I make the choices FOR ME and KEEP moving forward!! PERIOD and DONE DONE!!

I would love to say everything I have done for others has been appreciated. I have tons of supporters, but I cannot say that–I am sure of who they all are. I wish that I had the support from those I expect it from just as much as those I barely know. I wish these things like you do, but don't hold your breath that those people

What The Hell Happened
will change.

Some people cannot walk a mile in your shoes, and some will have a negative and judgmental stance on how I live my life. I have no regrets for my choices, but yes I would like things to be different in some areas. I would love effective communication with some people so they understand me better as a mother, cousin, wife, etc. But it is what it is, literally. I know I made choices that were right, and I never made a choice I feel I need to take back because of harm it caused intentionally, no.

When others reject my apologies for how they have felt about my decisions, I will always stand up for my mistakes. But that doesn't mean I regret my choice because I didn't. I learned to allow people to choose not to forgive me, and in those circumstances, I have to move on. Time keeps moving whether you are ready or not, and there is nothing else to do. I am not going to sit in a corner and cry, and I don't think you should beat on the door to get someone to believe you. I am gonna let it the HELL go.

If you are still debating on kicking them out, look at this. If they are cursing you out, disrespecting you, don't listen to you, or are not committed to growing up and doing better, look at that again. Look at yourself again, and dig deep into your soul. Are you a parent or a cream puff? Who is bending who over here?

You need to do some soul-searching because you are a cream puff. But if your friend or stranger talks to you like them, you are ready to fight. But you won't make them do nothing, so why you over here barking at me, and the people trying to help you?

They run their mouths and act like the boss, but you allow them to do that in your house. But those who are helping and trying to look out for you, you are ready to cuss out or kick them out. Something doesn't make sense here, so I had to say it another way. I still don't see it. Look at that again, Sis. This is not the road. I would rather have peace with less people than a lot of people bringing hell and disruption in my life. So I am done. I let it go!

Okay one more thing I have to say. Ya'll know me. As women, we are tempted to fix everything. If someone drops the ball, here we go as women, mothers, and wives to fix the situation and make things better.

I am telling you that you can empathize with them, you can hurt, you can go through all of the emotions BUT YOU DO NOT have to STALL there!! You do not have to be "Boo Boo the Fool." Stop losing sight of who you are as a woman because you are so busy trying to FIX everything!

I am telling you, if you are looking for a sign, this whole chapter was dedicated to YOU, and it is telling you that you need to LET IT GO! And the reason why is because you deserve some peace of mind, self-preservation, boundaries, and, most of all, some self-respect for the person who matters the most… YOU! We must understand that WE, as women, men, and even African-Americans, MUST put ourselves first and why because, without you, there will not be a strong family infrastructure.

What The Hell Happened

In my case, I will NOT have had my three daughters graduate from college with at least a Bachelor's degree. I wouldn't have traveled with a family of five to Africa twice if I lacked the discipline to achieve my goals. I am telling YOU that these things do NOT happen because I was liked by everyone or because I picked up the ball all the time when someone in my household dropped it. I LET some things GO, and I claimed it with authority!

I have no REGRETS, but I am happy about who I am and the person I have grown to be. See, this is what I am saying: YOU have to know YOU and WHO you are…once you know who you are - and what you want, dreams you have, goals you want to accomplish - there is NO penetrating that! Period!

So, what can you do with difficult people or situations that others can't get past? Don't let it guilt trip you no anymore. LET IT GO. Step out on faith, and do not be afraid!! Make your own rules and live up to it with the fullest intent! And let NO ONE dim your light or get in the way!

Yes, I mean even your children, husband, and whomever! I am living PROOF it can be done and you can live a life on your terms with no regrets being close to perfect! Hahah. But seriously, do you want this? Are you feeling me, and have you been picking up what I am putting down? Let's move on.

Financial Planning

Wake up! You are leaving here and living now, so do something. Go fund me is not a saving plan.

I know the topic many people in our neighborhoods dread to talk about is money! Funny thing, this is my favorite topic and I love to speak about it. I am just as bold in talking about money because of my relationship with money. Many people judge me and my respect for money and I don't care about their opinions deep down, but, for those that want to get to know me and how I can help the money factor in people's lives should know a few things.

I don't worship money, but I understand full well about what money can offer me. There are people who are okay with sitting on the couch talking about their bills, whining and complaining. I was never that person even when I was broke. I know, can you guess that Melvina was broke as a joke growing up?

Melvina W.

The truth about it, we always had money to provide, but growing up in the South didn't mean that much for black and brown people. When I say that I mean, dark and light brown black people. Growing up in Savannah Georgia was not a bad upbringing. I was raised in a Christian household by two loving parents. They were both married once and my brother and I were born into a loving home.

I did not say that the home was perfect–but I first learned respect while living here. I learned how to keep my mouth shut, how to stay out of grown folks business, and what it meant to disobey my parents. I was never big into the whopping thing or beating children with their clothes off. I felt that was too much and too close to slavery for me. I am not a slave and I never wanted my children to feel that way.

Yes, I wanted to raise my children differently but I never thought about respect being a negotiable factor. My father was the leader of the house and he led with the best information he had. He was a hard worker and often worked multiple jobs. He would be out at all hours it seemed working sun up to sun down to provide for us.

I remember him coming home and telling me to be better than my parents and so I looked at everything we did and started to analyze it. I didn't do this to judge my parents, but to understand what it meant to be better I needed to be honest about where we were. The good thing, we had a tight knit family. My family taught me the benefit first hand of having all your immediate family under one roof.

Financial Planning

I tell my daughters and any young girls I mentor to try and have a nuclear family if you can. This means to have all your children by the man you marry and fight like hell to stay together through the good and bad times. Staying together through thick and thin is not only good for your emotional wellbeing, it is also good for your money.

When you can build with someone, we all know basic math, two plus two equals four. If there are two people carrying their weight, that means you can move two or four times as fast. I wanted a partner that valued working hard like I did, but also working smarter. I wanted to marry someone who could put up the numbers like me and wasn't afraid to change our financial picture.

I remember when I was in my twenties and I was determined to buy a home. I talk more about this in my first book, but I said that I wanted to be a homeowner. I saw what my parents did to keep a roof over our heads and I knew the value of ownership rather than renting. When I own, I have an asset and not a liability. Learning the value of spending money that worked to build my wealth was one of the first lessons I learned. I refused to work my fingers to the bone so other people could enjoy my effort. I wanted to bake my cake and eat it too!

Homeownership was my first step toward financial freedom. I knew this was in the cards for me and I wanted a family to share it with me. I met Glenn at the perfect time because right around the time I bought my first house, we started getting close and one thing after another we were pregnant. I have some more to tell, but for now, stay with me. Being pregnant with our first child, moving into my house, and knowing that I was steering the ship to achieving my goals I felt empowered.

It was good that Glenn and I married about two almost three years later and we didn't marry because of the baby or anything. I needed real love - you hear me and that man knows how to put it down! So yes, committing to marriage, homeownership, and family was part of my foundation and relationship with money. How soon do we find out love and family with no money leads to problems?

I grew up with love, but the money was not as plentiful to go around. We had to stay on a budget, eat what was affordable, and travel as events and money allowed. I didn't want to suffer like that and travel on a budget. I wanted to travel first class and go to places outside the United States with my children. When I was growing up the furthest I went was up and down the East coast. I wanted more and I knew what that meant, more money.

I was grateful for what we had but I also knew, if I didn't want the same experience, I needed to do something different. Getting my degrees and advancing my education was one of the best investments I made into me. I was determined to get a Bachelor's degree.

Only after I got that, I knew it wouldn't be enough so I kept going to school to increase my value. Money isn't just about what you earn, it is also about

Financial Planning

what you invest. Spending money and investing are two different things.

I always want to be a wise investor and people who want to keep money make it a habit to make everything work for their favor more than one time. Even if I had the money, I believe in wearing things more than once. If I buy something, I have plans for it and it is not just to be cute. I am cute already, I want it to bring me more money. If I get a phone, I want to know how I am going to make money with the phone. If I buy a car, a house, and anything else, it has to make money sense.

Catch me drift? I know you might say Melvina, "Do you see everything as a money transaction?" I want to tell you like this–I could say "Absolutely Yes." but it would not sum up all I want to say, so I want to take it piece by piece so you quote me correctly. I do believe money is the answer to getting anything you want.

If you want a family, you will need it. To buy a house, car, take a vacation, you will need it, to have the best healthcare, you will need it. To pay for college for you and your children, you will need it, to invest in your future like retirement, you will need it. Hell, a dead person who has already died need money to be buried.

Money is an equalizer and we all need it so we do need to be mindful about it. I know in our communities we don't like talking about money because most of us don't have it and are hesitant to believe we can get it and some of us are NOT going to get it in this lifetime. I believe the word says that the poor will always be poor or something like that, right? We are often feeling content with not having enough, having less, or finding an excuse for why we can't rub two nickels together. Keep in mind, I used to be one of those people too, briefly - that couldn't rub two nickels together - BUT never content. .

I had to rob Peter to Pay Paul. I got the free hook ups in the hood and did what I could to skate by when I thought I had too. I quickly learned, sitting in the dark with no lights, or lights and no water, was getting old. I didn't want to raise my daughters in an unstable environment and my husband Glenn didn't either. We needed a strong financial base which neither one of us came from. Then when we had the twins, we had double duty and very little help.

Our parents loved us but they didn't live with us. We had to come up with a financial plan that we could win with. It had to take care of the bills, our vacations, permit our dreams, and move things along in other areas of our lives. I feel like financial freedom–for me, is having enough money to pay for all your bills and some until the time you think you will die. The common age of life is in your seventies and eighties. This is a long time to live and a lot of money to save.

The prices of goods are only going up so to stop working too soon would be a grave miscalculation I cannot afford. I don't accept no's as you know, so for whatever I want in life I need to make a winning plan to get it done. Retirement is one of those things too. I have a goal to ensure I have enough money when I stop working to pay for the quality of life I live now. I don't

Financial Planning

want to ball out now and be impoverished later. I want to stabilize my life the same way I did for my children.

I am not the parent sitting around expecting my children to take care of me. I know some parents put this pressure on their kids to take care of them, but what if they don't? What about all these children struggling to take care of themselves?

You think I am going to sit around and hope my children take care of me to be financially set to retire? Pleaseeeee! I am out here grinding because Melvina will make a way for what I need Come Hell or High Water. If you are banking on people to take care of you, you better let that the hell go!

Before you can think about the future, many of you need to focus on the here and now. When I first started this journey to financial freedom, I knew I had to save up 6 to 9 months of living expenses for extenuating circumstances. Life happens, you can get sick, fired, or have to close down. The reason doesn't matter so much, the result is the same, you have to survive. So plan for what can happen.

For some of you lucky people you can get a whole life policy that can allow you to get insurance on your life, your job, or income. If you can get it, get it. Don't wait to get it because you might not qualify. I personally don't qualify but I don't use that as an excuse for why I don't have the same thing I would tell anybody else. When you hear a no, you don't accept it, you find how you can get it done under the circumstances.

Melvina W.

I knew when I was denied that I needed to ensure I had the money to cover the expenses up ahead. I knew I needed to have what I needed to take care of my parents if they needed me too, along with myself, my husband, and my children. I am thinking about all of that and you should too. In our community we need to stop waiting until hell breaks loose and then do the talking. The savings, or the shopping.

I don't know why we wait until we can't do something to have a taste to get it done. We need to do better with jumping on stuff early so we have the most options in life. I remember when I had my first job making 40k a year. I knew it wasn't enough real quick. I needed to make at least 100K just to get my bills in check and work to make my house an asset and not a liability.

The biggest problem I see with us is not being able to make the decisions we need to find the money. If you are broke, you need to look at what you can cut to find the money. When I hear people tell me they can get $50 to start this or buy that, I don't know how to act because I don't understand it. Not because I haven't been there, but if I need $50 a day, I am gonna do something to make that money everyday no matter what.

We are too lax with failing to reach our financial goals. We can see we don't make enough to buy something and then make no plans on how we can bring it in reach. We could charge rent here, stop going out, quick shopping, and etc to find the money. The problem is most of us won't take a temporary loss in areas to afford stuff we like or need.

Financial Planning

I had this woman tell me that I wasn't like her so she wasn't including me in her question. Of course I asked, "What do you mean I am not like you?" She replied, "Well, it's just you don't know what it's like not to have $50." I looked her in the face and I said, "What you mean to say I am not dumb enough to have a Louis Vuitton bag on my arm if I cannot find $50." How is it you cannot get $50 per day but you are standing there with a Louis Vuitton bag, fake nails, eye lashes, toes done, hell you even got a shower but you broke!

If I do not have any money I am working two jobs, barely sleeping, and I might not have time to shower either. I am about getting it "DONE DONE" - Come Hell or High Water and NO excuses I had about why I can't, I gotta let it go. I refused to fail. The reason I am not like her wasn't because of how much money I had compared to her. It was how I freaking think compared to how she thinks. She has a poverty mindset, worse than a scarcity mindset.

A poverty mindset would buy expensive bags, cars, jewelry, dinners, and all when you don't have a savings plan. That is not about scarcity, this is about making decisions that will leave you in tha' poor house, broke as a joke and I don't give a doggone. When people like that try to judge me I am quick to cut them off, because their real problem is not my success but their problem with money and their mindset. Like I tell anybody, I love money, I love me, I love my husband, my girls, and my life. I love these things - there is no stopping that, this train is moving on. They are paramount in my life, so I make time for them.

Melvina W.

Whatever you really want bad enough you make plans for how you are going to get it. When people don't take the time to focus and make plans for what they want, I don't sit around and help them figure it out either. I am not the type of person to contribute to a person's go fund me for anything if I know they did nothing to prevent it. So many people use that platform as I screwed up bail me out money it aint funny and not to mention the fraudulent reason, setting up a go fund me to pay a bill that you have every month, really?

I am sure the platform has great use, I really am. But so many people use that site to beg for money they know they should have planned for. I am not your fall woman and I am not going to pay a bill that I didn't enjoy racking up. You wanted to go out here and smoke up your life, drink yourself dead, and do all this stuff to cut your life short and you never thought about life insurance? And if you didn't, why should I have to pay to bury you? Hell, why should anybody?

I told you, when you love your money, you love options. When people think, family, friends–probably soon not no more, ask me to give up what I worked for because they stopped caring about their life, I tell them the same thing they told themselves. "I'm good." I know people think I am harsh, right. But think about this with me and tell me for real, doesn't it make sense.

If you worked your job. You brought home a paycheck. The amount doesn't matter. The rules are there for what you should do with your money. Put some here in savings, put a percentage to bills, investment/retirement, groceries, and whatever else you need.

Financial Planning

You can even have a budget for stuff for you too so you can get it all in there. If you have to put your pants on one leg at a time like me, why should I give you something I worked for and you didn't?

I can empathize with parents losing babies and young children. I support March of Dimes because I had preemies with my twins and it is not easy. It can be scary to see your babies in the Neonatal Intensive Care unit (NICU). The last thing you want to think about is how much this all costs, you have to focus on them getting well. It makes sense and I support that, but I am not going to give my money to nobody who I feel could have done better with their lives.

Does that make me a judge? Well, I guess so. It makes me a judge of what I will and won't do with my money. I am not going to give it away for something dumb, I worked too hard. And I am not going to give away my nest egg to end up with nothing while others make out like a fat rat. I am not "Boo Boo the Fool."

I am going to put my money where it grows. If you cut out most of the money you spend or give away to people who are not an investment, you could have enough to buy a rental property. Write your book, start a business, or invest in stocks and other assets. It is time to start seeing your future as something you are responsible for. Nobody owes you anything, and what you want to have in life is ultimately your decision.

What I will never understand is how several people can live together and never buy nothing. Why are you working and getting all this money to give it

Melvina W.

away? Renting is wasting your money and it doesn't make sense to me. You cannot sell and get money from something you don't own.

I know someone who has a son who is renting from them. He is content with buying his Air Jordan's, smoking weed, and seeing his mother struggle just as much now as when she was younger. Nothing is changing there in that picture.

I don't believe in the crappy excuse that you cannot buy a house because of the economy and this or that. I know someone who bought a house for $1 because they knew how to write grants. So if there's a will, there is a way. Where there is an excuse for those too lazy to work and get it, they will find one.

I don't feel sorry for people who don't buy. I ask where did your money go? If you make 30k or 40k a year, that is 80k every two years. If you live and work for 40 years that is over a million dollars. How you don't have anything to show for all that time and money?

Tell me how this makes any kind of sense. This is wasteful spending, and not given a doggone how things are going, you will miss the mark. It's a huge disconnect to see people who are financially poor but have all these expensive things in life. All I can say is not in my house. If money is tight, there is only one train of thought: survival. We are not trying anything else on for size. We are not window shopping. We are zeroing in on how we are going to make it out.

Financial Planning

There is no sense in driving the finest car with no garage to put it in. Why are luxury cars in an apartment complex? Can you explain that to me? If you got a luxury car, you should be able to buy a house. I had to ask myself some serious questions.

When my daughters were young, I would never buy them Air Jordans and things like that if the rest of our lives weren't set. I wasn't looking at going on vacations unless my entire family could go. Why are we paying for cell phones and NOT for education or to start our own business? You can give your child a Limited Liability Company (LLC) for the price some people are spending on shoes! This is what we have to LET GO....

I am not saying budgeting is easy. I remember when the bills were 3K, and we were only bringing in 2K. What budget? Life was hard, and decisions had to be made and plans implemented. It meant I didn't get sex some nights.

I worked remotely and away from home for months and weeks at a time. But you best believe when we started making money, like 10k a month, and the bills were 5k a month, budgeting was a piece of cake. We were saving and rejoicing about it. Our thought process and MY unit of discipline and focus pushed me, and I made sure that that lesson filtered down to everyone up in my house.

I know I ain't the only one who loves money. You can be shy but I have family members who were not shy about asking me for money. When I was broke as a joke, I had several cousins who formed a group to swap money to help each of us out. She would give me $800 this month to pay whatever bill that was in dire need…and then next month, I would give her back her $800 with an extra whatever amount to cover her bills. We were "Robbing Peter to pay Paul" and doing that over and over for a minute.

Now, we are both in our own lane, making things happen. And those days are gone, for real. I have been approached by family members, mostly cousins, who still say, "Hey cousin, let me hold something." I would ask how much they needed, and here they go with some ghetto-fied mess. "I need $107.36 to pay my light bill (electricity)." I NEVER once had someone ask me for money to start a business, to invest, or do nothing that led to more money. All of it was to pay a debt of some kind. Tell me that is not sad.

If we had friends with money, many of us would have nothing to bring for them to consider. We would blow the reason it is good to know billionaires. I give money when I can or when I Felt Like it. I am not given out money just because people ask me. It has to be something I want to do, and I usually don't expect it back. But I don't let no one play me for a fool. I am not going to keep giving the same ole' excuse.

I believe in making good decisions and being generous, but I will never be anyone's fool! It might seem SMART to them to keep asking for money because they are relying on your kindness and hoping you are dumb. Nothing wrong with helping someone out here and there, but all the time or on a consistent basis

Financial Planning

like they are a bill, nope! Let it Go!

The best way to get out of the sinking money pit with people is to be very direct. I ain't never scared, and I have the balls to say how I feel and mean what I say. If I say "no" I mean that. If you have the balls to ask me for money, then you have the balls to get "told" however I feel, and whatever I am going to give you is an example of my generosity.

I can't stand when someone tries to judge what you are giving them as if it is not enough when they don't have a dame penny or pot to piss in. So, I clearly state my answer, and how they take it is up to them. If it is an offer with stipulations, that can like it or not, take it or leave I don't care.

I can tell you that any problem they have with my answer is their problem, not mine. I didn't ask them for money, they asked me. I have a right to protect my money and spend it how I want to. I don't explain how I am going to use it or why my answer is "no" when I say "no." I always stand on business, and I will speak how I feel. I am no mouse, and I am very vocal about what I care about, and my money, qualifies as an area of high importance.

Someday, we will all leave this place, and you cannot take money with you. I understand that very well. This is why I encourage people to enjoy their money and be smart about it. It is not smart to spend all your money "living" if that means you have to borrow to die. I will never understand why people will expect people who didn't give you $10 while you lived, to pay

Melvina W.

$10k to bury you when you die.

This is just not good sense, and I don't have the patience to care about what others don't. Yes, I would bury my parents if I had to, but if I knew that, why wouldn't I get a policy to help me pay for it? It is stupid to me the way we'll live our lives as if we will never die, and when we do, it's somebody else's problem.

Most families skip family events; I know I do. I don't spend any money on them because I don't see the purpose of gathering to talk about nothing. I don't want to gather where things will be a drag, and about people complaining about why things aren't going well in their lives.

If that's all you have to give, you are not giving me nothing to work with. If things were different, I might come to family outings and better support, but family don't get a pass at tapping me dry financially. Family is the fastest way to grow broke, you heard me.

It gets "real cutthroat" for me dealing with family because I have seen what it does to people. I know what they think when they see me. They smell money because they see me traveling around the world, and they feel like I am doing something they are NOT doing. That I have something more than what they have.

Yet, we are in the same family and have the same opportunities. I just made a decision about what I am going to do with both! Too many of the people that would ask to hang out wanted something from me, and I don't mean friendship. They don't think that they can

Financial Planning

achieve what I have, so they come begging for stuff, and I don't want to entertain that. Those who think let me see what I can get from her or have that kind of attitude, I dismiss.

I don't listen to people who don't have anything to say. I don't entertain them. I don't go where they go, and the word NO comes out a lot around those people. It can get abrasive real quick. I am not sure why people think they are entitled to tell you how to spend what you saved, worked for, and did what you needed to do to make it.

People with broken mentalities don't last around me, and there is NO conversation to be had. I let them go. I make and solve my OWN problems. Someone else's problems are NOT mine and will NOT be mine!

You have to set boundaries if you want to have money. No boundaries, means your money is going to go out in every direction, and you won't know what is coming or going. I don't operate like that.

Years ago, I set boundaries with my family. At first, I wondered if I was too harsh, but it got easier and easier to let it go. For those with NOTHING to work with, there is no conversation either. If you got something of substance, knowledge, a concise plan, growth development or even some kind of funk to throw on something, then we got something to talk about.

Please keep in mind all we are doing is talking. I do not do business with my family that is disastrous!! Sorry to say, not everyone is cut out for starting their own business. Some of you are straight employees, so go get the job, work the job, keep the job, and be happy!!

I don't recommend getting it to squabbles about finances. I don't loan money or ask for money anymore– those days are gone!! Any ghetto-fied BS that they got going on is for them, and I stay clear of it. I am loud and direct about who and what I am and whether they even qualify to be in my circle. I can tell you NOW I have no regrets for the family members I had to let go.

I don't love anyone more than what I got going on and I don't expect anything different from others. This is the way the world works, and if you are out here with your hand out begging for stuff, don't be surprised if you come away with nothing. This is a free country and we all can achieve great things and reap the rewards of hard work. I think it is funny when people think I am going to feel guilty or go through a guilt trip because they broke. I don't, and I am not.

People get into the situation they are in because of their choices. If people call me selfish, I would agree with them. I am selfish and I do care about myself. And here is why, "What would caring about them do for me? How would that benefit me? Would I get further in life because I helped them or talked to them?"

You and I both know that the answer is no. So why am I going to feel bad? If they call me a narcissist, I've heard that too, and it is okay with me. I will worry about me, and they can worry about them. I know how

Financial Planning

I am going to be living over here. I can't speak for anybody else. So, if I were you and people want you to feel guilty about helping them, you better let it go. They will be alright and if you got your money, you will be too. That's why they want to be your friend anyway.

I openly let them know that whatever they think I am they can keep on thinking it. And the truth of the matter is I have LET GO of any preconceived notions about me that are designed to TRY to hurt me or bring me down to their level! Because when we get down to the heart of the matter, they don't shop where I shop. They don't go where I go. They don't have the infrastructure setup the way I do at this day and time. We are on two different wavelengths, and I am not going to explain my moves to people who can't make them.

If you get it, you get it. If you don't, you don't. Again, not my problem. You have to know what problems are yours and what battles are yours to fight. There are things I have accomplished that others are still dreaming about. I am 100% clear about who I am! There is NOTHING you can tell me about me that I do not know already!! So I don't deal with anyone or anything that is NOT for me! Period.

If you can pick up something from what I just put down, grab it, and let's keep moving on.

When people drop the ball, I don't pick it up. NO life insurance, you don't have the money to bury them because you, too, don't have insurance. So they will have to understand they will have the cheapest funeral possible. Let It Go.

Melvina W.

Don't let your feelings get caught up. Three weeks trying to bury your family member by setting up a GoFundMe and begging for money to bury your loved one. Really? Cremation is not what you want, but you have no plot, no tombstone, and you are not planning for it.

How does this make sense? Why do we do this? We can't bury someone else when we are not thinking of nothing. Stop wasting money on the dead.

Even Jesus said let the dead bury the dead. It means those who are living should plan to live. When you die, while you lived, you should have planned for that because you can't when you are dead. See how that works? Don't put the burden on your family or GoFundMe.

Put it on yourself. See your mom and make a policy. Stop being lazy and blaming people. Stop putting it on the public; take responsibility. We know this stuff, but we choose to blindly follow along and do nothing.

If you got money, then do right by your parents because you made provision; that is what children do. We are to carry each other, but we need to learn and do better going forward. If everything is free, how will you elevate? Where did your taxes go? Why are you not investing and doing the right thing?

Financial Planning

When they Say No

Keep in mind that "I Didn't Say It Was Over!" I say "yes" to me all the time, but that doesn't mean people don't tell me "no." I hear no, just like everyone else, and gotta deal with it. I gotta be honest. Hearing "no" is not a common occurrence. Having money gives you options, privileges, and helps you get stuff done.

I don't cut my own grass because I pay someone else to do it. I don't clean my house every day. I pay someone else to do it. I don't run every part of my business on a daily basis because, yes, I pay someone else to do it. I don't even drive myself around all the time because I have a driver who I pay to do it.

    I like these options because that means I can focus on what I do best and afford these things. I love my options and I like hearing yes. If I hear no, I am looking for a way to make that no a yes. You best believe it, unless it isn't something I want. I am not going to accept no if I don't have to either.

    I know other people feel like they have to deal with hearing no, but I believe in getting what you make plans for. I remember saying I wanted to skydive in the book I Didn't Say It Was Over. I was told by the pilot I couldn't do it because of my weight. I heard him, but I also heard me.

    This is something I want to do. So I am either going to find someone who will tell me yes, or I will do what I need to do at some point to get a yes. I will not accept no as an answer.

    When I was told I couldn't get whole life insurance from one company, I Didn't Say It Was Over, and stopped there. I kept looking and found a company that could accommodate what I wanted. Now, do I sometimes have to pay more for what I want, yes. Good thing I got more money. Money is a tool, and we all need it. I am upfront about it, and I respect it. Yes, I make plans for what I want and ensure I do whatever I need to to get it.

    If I have to shake a leg and show some ass, I will do that too but trust and believe millions of dollars would have to be on the table. These are some high-priced legs, and even though this is a flat-dimpled butt I have, when cleaned up right, it is very expensive. But Glenn would have a fit if I shook it anywhere else other than his direction.

We have an understanding there, so I have boundaries, and I know what I will and won't do. I refused to be limited in my mindset or how I like to move. I like shopping in the stores I like, flying first class, and doing things the Melvina way. But let me be clear: I don't want money to be your excuse to not have ambition to obtain more.

I didn't come from a rich family or have a silver spoon in my mouth. I have to put my pants on one leg at a time every day like you. I have to work. Some of the work you have to do first is free of charge. You need to call people, apply, fill out applications, and talk to people. You cannot sit on the couch and think everything is going to come to you. It will not; you have to go get it!

Melvina's Quote:
Persistence and tenacity are very important! You should never quit, never surrender unless you are dead! And even then, you should wake the hell up!

You need to formulate a plan for how you are going to get things done. When I had no money, I made time to figure things out to get it. Don't waste your time worrying about bills. They are going to come and go, and you aren't going to change that. But if you spend your time planning how you are going to fix things, get things back, make the money you need, and be there for

Melvina W.

those you love. Now, you have given me something to work with!

Too many people do not think about solving their problems; they only live within their limited means. You must change that thinking if you want more out of life. For free, you can also put together financial goals. You need something to work toward, and when I started, I hardly had any money in the bank during those times in my life. So be prepared for the ups and the downs, and don't beat yourself up. But also, don't get comfortable and formulate a million excuses for why you don't have something going.

Starting over can be a beast, but we all may have to do it. Start looking at what you can do in the next six months to a year to change this aspect of your life. I make sure that if I hear a no to something I want, the no is not forever. All hope is not lost because I do not operate that way or believe that. You are NOT dead YET!

So when I hear a no, it is only no for the moment. I am busy working on the other moments to see what I can make happen to make a possibility and a reality the yes I am looking for. I have a made-up mind that I will hear a yes come hell or high water for the things I value, and I would encourage anyone to have that mentality to make it in life.

A good example of when I turned a no into a yes was when I had children. I needed to get out of debt. It was a road that I know we have all been on. Where we have more going out than coming in, and we see the issue but we are not able to solve it. You won't believe what I had to do to help dig my family out of the dirt!

I didn't sit on my hands and look at others to bail me out, I learned early on that I needed to be able to do this for myself. I had to not only get a second job, but a third job also. I worked three jobs and slept like four hours a day and ate food on the go to make ends meet. My husband stepped up and put on the apron to cook and do the cleaning while I made the money in coding to bring our family out.

My husband and I are in love, but we think differently. My work ethic is different from his and not in a comparison way. So, while he is working one job and wearing the apron, I am working three jobs and bringing home the bacon!!!

We are a team and it took the both of us to do what we do. I am grateful for his sacrifice and our partnership to raise our daughters and achieve what we have thus far in life. We both own properties we purchased. He has the ability to be self-sufficient if he likes and so do I. We both valued being able to say what we have accomplished and what we want. He can buy what he wants as long as he pays his half of the bills and I do the same. We are 50/50 partners.

I don't have those old-school ways that women have to be in the kitchen cooking and cleaning and that other BS. I am a woman, a great wife and mother, and no, I don't believe that means stepping back into the 30s. My job was to pull away from anything that distracted me from the goal. So, I never got caught up with petty things like getting my nails or hair done. I was not an over spender when going to the mall; I focused on what we needed. With groceries, I kept it simple but effective.

Any bill I could reduce or get rid of, I did with a quickness. I got rid of car payments and other monthly subscriptions that were not helping our goals. I remember when our daughters were young, they used to watch the VHS tapes when we stopped having cable. As we advanced in life, I got cable and recently just got rid of it. Look at how times have changed!

It took being strong in my mind and will to focus on my dreams long enough to accomplish them. I know I am headstrong, absolutely! I am strong-minded, aggressive, and all that because I need strength to survive. I go against the current of water and make it change directions to make sure I get what I want to accomplish.

Someone telling me NO doesn't stop me, especially if the person I am saying no to is not even on my level. Some people can go left, and I am NOT following them, I go right. So, I will cautiously tell you to know your audience cause some people are NOT worth listening to, to even tell them, "No, I will not do that."

I have to say this again to those in the back, "What have they done?" You ever think why are they saying NO to you? No, you cannot think like that. Why? Because thinking about you means you are not bailing them out no more? Or is it because thinking for you means you can outdo them or move on without

When they Say No them?

You gotta let it go that being selfish or worrying about you is not good or healthy. It is unhealthy to neglect what you want and only please others. There, I said it. Why is it always you who has to hear no when you constantly say yes to everything?

I get asked sometimes, "Is it good to always hear yes?" I confidently reply, "As a matter of fact, it is because that means I am getting what I want. That means I have put things in place to make it possible. That means this train is moving forward no matter what. It means I have unlimited options, and this NO word is NOT gonna stop me."

I set up the infrastructure no matter what to make no's turn to yes'. I have education and critical thinking skills to ensure I can conquer whatever I need to face. I have money to throw at situations because sometimes that's what it takes to ensure things are taken care of. So, what was the question again, is it good to always hear yes? Hell yeah!!

What's the nugget that you need to get from me, my mindset is how I have accomplished a lot and also protected myself from a lot. I used to wear my heart on my sleeve, and I got tired of being taken advantage of and left for dead. I heard no like you do, but I had to find a way for it not to feel like a roadblock I couldn't get around.

If you can't get around it, I can tell you that one major roadblock that is present is IN your mind! You are a slave of your own making. Your freaking mind is taking you hostage because somehow you believe that NO is all there is and all you can do.

I wrote this book to help people get out of this stuck-in-neutral thinking and encourage them to let it go. Let things go that hold you strapped because you are being caged or rather stuck in your mind, money, and the way you treat others haven't been helping you before. If you want to change your life, you need to make changes for how you think, spend money, spend your time, and how you give to others. Not everyone deserves your best or resources. Some people deserve a peace sign and to see your smoke drive off into the sunset because it is over.

So, if you have had no creative ideas, no innovative planning or thoughts - just, "Oh well, they said No, I can not do it." You need to let it go. That thinking is going to keep you stuck for decades to come, and in fact, this book can't help you, you can just close it.

If you don't want nothing, there is nothing I can do for you or help you with. No, my mind doesn't hear the word NO, and if it slips up and hears it. I push back and ignore it because I will turn it into a yes, come hell or high water, for the things that I WANT. For sure, I know YOU can turn a NO into at least a not right now, or not at this moment, like it is just a matter of when you hear, perhaps!

Sometimes, you need to expand your vision. You might want to marry someone who doesn't want you, and they told you no. But that doesn't mean you can't get married. You just got the wrong guy. Keep building and making plans for what you want: to be married. Stop focusing on the little details that can change. In finding a yes, it doesn't mean your plans won't be adjusted some to get the yes.

I am a married woman with a family, and it would not be my intention to get a yes if it would harm my husband or children. I care about them and they are in my plans and heart. I want to see them win and pray they want the same for me. If they don't, they will come on board soon because my show won't stop. But I will never do something to violate our partnership and family bond for the sake of getting a yes to something.

There are times when a no is the answer. It is a no when I no longer want something or it doesn't align with my husband, family, and other goals. I know how to be a team player even though I am usually the captain. I have a strong direction and will, but I am not railroading anyone into something they don't want.

I cannot make someone tell me yes if they have said no. I want to be clear: things I want for myself I do go and get. But for things that include the participation of another party, you may have to respect someone else's no.

Regardless of whether it is my children or a company that has decided to put me on ice, I analyze the situation and determine what Melvina wants. You best believe the employer is looking out for the company, and I am doing the same. I suggest working to build with a company that can see your value the same as with people. If people can not see what you bring or are not picking up what you are putting down, start looking at bettering yourself to increase your options.

Staying at one job for twenty and thirty years is dead. People are trying to move up, make more money, and live the life they want to. We don't have the time to wait around for people to come around if another company is ready to put you where you want to be right now. I won't be forced to guess and wait to see what is going to happen. I see the writing on the wall, and I start preparing for what's to come next. It's simple for me, and I trust it will be the same for you too.

The mindset I have to make a no into a yes started really when I was a young girl telling my parents I was going to have a maid and a driver. They thought I was joking or just messing around, but I was dead serious. I didn't expect to work my fingers to the bone doing work that didn't amount to what I wanted to make.

I wanted to work smarter and not harder, unlike my dad, who worked harder and not always smarter. I understood the assignment to do better than him when he told me. I knew that when he found out what I was going to do as a business owner and medical coder, he knew my plan was a YESSS and good enough for him.

I remember when I paid the last payment on my student loans. I paid for my own college myself with loans. I know a lot of people repeatedly complain about having to pay for school, but I did it. I paid for an education that I knew would pay me back so I could pay

When they Say No

off the debt. The problem too often with people is they want degrees that don't pay them back. Acting is great for the 1 percent that makes it. But for everyone else, it is a whole lot of debt for you to go and be a waiter somewhere.

I refused to take on debt that wasn't smart, and if you are looking at going back to school, make it make sense. Don't be out here getting no degree in business when that means you are going to be a manager on your feet all day, making 60k a year or something like that. There are people without a degree getting over 100k, so why? I have medical coders who finish my medical coding school, making 70k a year.

It is not hard to make money, but it is hard to have the mindset to make money and work for it. I think the biggest no most people hear is not from other people but from within themselves. They say no, I cannot make it. No, I don't have enough. No, I am not smart enough, blah blah blah. If you think like that, you will have exactly what you say, NOTHING. I will not have anything to help a person who has a defeated mindset on everything before they even try. Dr. Lee might be able to help you, but I cannot.

Melvina W.

I am not afraid to say no. There is only a handful of people that will have me compromise with saying no and that is my husband and children. That list is very short because not everyone should have that much impact on what you do. Too many jobs will cut you loose and close the doors without telling you.

I cannot tell you how often I have seen people out in the cold because a company was inconsiderate. I refused to be one of those people, so I always try to keep other things going because you never know. You should have more than one way of making your money because your bills won't stop because life happens. That is what savings is for.

It can be scary for some people to make decisions because they don't have a savings plan, so they stay in pitiful situations. I don't think it is smart to quit a job. Let yourself get fired if you can and collect unemployment, or if you don't got another job waiting on you. YES, I will let a job go if they are acting like they are on crack and treating me like a slave. Oh yes, that job gotta go!!

However, I have a replacement for the income or money in the bank or somewhere! I know how to

When they Say No

hold my peace long enough to get what I need! It is not the end of the world because you hear a no or you speak a no to yourself. I will not work a job that makes me feel like I cannot catch my breath or they own me. I like a good challenge but I will not be bullied. I am a grown woman, and I won't be treated like I am less than or like I don't know my worth, especially in the Health Information Management arena!

When I had to pay my dues, I did that. If a company thought I should have given more, I expect more money. I work to the job description, and if I go above that it is because I see something I want beyond that. Show me the MONEY. We are not on jobs to be friends or family; they want their work done, and I want to collect my MONEY. We have an understanding, and when we don't, it's time for me to go.

They can think I am mean or money-hungry, I don't care. They don't pay my bills, and if I needed help I wouldn't imagine any of them offering to give me something. So why should I give something to them? I deal just fine with the rules, considering I am very secure with the person I am. I know my value, and I know where I am going and where I have been.

For those who think I am mean, if mean is the only word you can come up with for me, I am good with that! Trust and believe because I am a born leader and a woman. A lot of people are not ready - but you will get ready come hell or high water because I didn't say it was over. I will let you go!

I don't work for free. If people want my expertise, for me to mentor them or teach them what I know, show me the MONEY, and I will make time. When people spend their money for what they want, it also weeds out the people who are wasting time. I don't like to waste my time because I can't get it back. I love to talk to people and help, but I won't waste my time speaking into thin air. I want people who can pick up what I am saying and get to work and change their life!

Annnnndddddd I must add I am not afraid of what people say about me. I know some people turn their no's into yes' because they are afraid of what others think. Not me. I won't be bullied into saying yes, and I will only agree if I mean it. I am way past people telling me that I say NO too much. Remember, I clearly know my audience, and most people who feel this way say yes too much. Not my circle and not my kind of people. This is not a person of substance for me!

I look at people and ask, "What are they working with?" Probably nothing! I like a good challenge when people want to compare apples to apples, but they have to have something going on to give me something to work with. For many, nope, they don't have anything but opinions! Some people trying to tell me what I give and don't give is such a little point, and I would probably be deaf 100% on them. Because I am notorious for being sarcastic and flipping on them and asking, "How is that YES you've been saying all the time working out?"

Tell me, what houses you own, what places have you traveled to, and what surplus of money are leftover in your bank account after all the bills are paid? What generational wealth have you accumulated? Has all of your children completed college - student-loan-free? I ain't playing with people! I ain't never scared.

Listen, you can stop reading if this doesn't make sense, OR it is NOT your cup of tea!! Hell, stop reading NOW. Cause if you don't like generational wealth, building assets by investment properties, retirements, being student loan free, paying bills, and traveling first class. You are right; I am not your cup of tea. If you are NOT feeling this kind of situation, like it is not enough, means I am clearly NOT the person for you. You need to LET ME GO!!!

The same way, I am prepared to fire those who cannot give me a yes for what I need, and I am paying a service, I don't blame you for letting me go with a quickness, too. If I ask someone to do something that I am paying for and they are saying no, I need to find someone else who can tell me yes. I am not shy, and I don't hold my tongue. I fired my social media guy and told him I was going to do it because he failed at his job. I am a great customer. I pay my bills on time. BUT I will not be taking advantage of or robbed blind.

I let it go, I let them go, and if people let me go, I do understand. Of course, there are people in my life and relationships that I do want to hold on to. My husband, for one, is a relationship that I built to keep and cultivate. You best believe if I say yes, we are going to come around to the yes, but we do talk it out. We have a partnership.

Now, with the three beautiful daughters we bore

Melvina W.

and raised together, I am not their friend or homegirl so what I said goes in my household. I know it is like I am a tyrant or a dictator. I didn't apologize for what I said because I meant it. Still do, BUT that doesn't mean I don't have unconditional love for them. They tell me no today all the time, but they are doing it from their houses. They earned the right to make their own decisions, and I respect their wishes. It's nice being the boss and saying what you will and will not tolerate. They get that from me!

What I will do until my last breath is love, my daughters and my husband. They have my unconditional love and it will always be there no matter their no's or yes' towards me. I am going to be Melvina, and I would like for this feeling to be mutual, even though I know sometimes it is not. That is not my problem, but some things are their choice, and people can change. I have changed my ways in some areas when absolutely necessary, and I compromise here and there, but it is out of my choice.

No one is holding a gun up to anybody's head and making them do anything they don't want to do. I am not going to hold on to old things and the past. I want to move forward, and I say no to that. But I will never say no to loving my daughters and being there for them how I can. When I say yes, my yes is a yes. I have done the damn thang. I have been married for 26 years and in love with the same man for 29 years. I raised three daughters, all college-educated and living on their own. I am a businesswoman, making my own money and taking care of myself.

When they Say No

They are still wet behind the ears, and their thoughts are what they are today. Life has a way of showing us all something that they, too will learn. We all learn as we get older and wiser. We will always need our mother and somebody to help guide us through life. I am glad to be that for my daughters when they need me. In the meantime, I am doing what I want in life and not worried about the choices they make because they are grown. I LET THEM GO!

You will have to let your children go also and allow them to grow up to be the women or the men you raised them to be. Don't handicap them or baby them because you are not doing them no favors. The world is tough, but they should be built for it if you did your job. If you didn't, try to do it now. There is still time. Let's move on.

It's just business. Tenure doesn't matter when you are looking at indispensability. Build your wealth. Increase your mind. Stop being small-minded. A 401k, 60K or 50K a year job is not enough for you to retire, especially if you are late in the game.

DO you know how much bread and butter cost today? Do you really think that having less than 500k to retire will be okay? Two plus two is four. Prices are going up, and they are not going down no matter who is in office. We are looking for someone to save us and keep us coddled and wrapped up in a blanket of lies.

We have to let it go! Let the old things pass away. Irrevocable trust, 401k, life insurance, and accountant, bank accounts are all something you need.

Melvina W.

What about when people say no? We find another way. I didn't say this was over. Let go of the excuses! Let go of the people saying No when God already said yes! I want to go skydiving, but they said no. I need to be 225 pounds. I will find a way around that.

I just have to spend more, and I know that. I say what I want, and I get it come hell or high water. That is because I value what I want to do. DO you value your words? Do they carry weight? Is your word your bond, or is it some random thing?

Some of us are limited because we hold back. Stop holding back. Find someone who loves you for you. If you can, get in the bed and let it go. Have an Explosion of passion. Wet the bed with your excitement and fall into a deep sleep! It is a way of waking up your senses and helping you to achieve the most.

When they Say No

Release Your Passion - Enjoy Sex

If you know anything about me, you will know I enjoy sex. I don't apologize for talking and being loud about it. I know I surprise people when I do, and I like that, too. I think sex should be talked about openly, especially with married women, because we got married into this. This is one of the best things to come out of the partnership of marriage.

Why is it that women feel they cannot be honest with their husbands about what they need? I am going to tell you right now: I didn't do anything with anybody unless I felt they were worth it. I am not talking about their size and what they had going on. I was looking at what they did for me and what they could bring to the table first. They had to work to get close to me.

For these women out here giving it up for a compliment and paying a little bill here and there. Girl, you betta look at your inventory again. If you are only worth a $100 phone bill and a compliment, you have more problems than you know. I am not doing anything with no one if they cannot see my worth or I see nothing in them to work with.

    I was quick to tell someone this is not gonna work out, and we were a long way from doing anything. I wasn't trying to waste my time with men focusing on a point system; I wasn't going to be another tick on their box. I had to be the priority. I am a QUEEN, and I have always been. The man that was going to make it into my heart and my panties had to bring it, or nothing was happening.

    For the ladies that say he got to be fine before you can wink an eye or show a little leg. I get it. I don't want no bugger bear, either. I knew that the man I wanted to have had to be packing more than what was in his pants and having a handsome face. I am not a shallow woman, and I need depth to keep me interested. I am glad to say I am a woman of standards and attraction.

    If I don't feel an attraction or see you as a friend, I was quick to friendzone. I am sure you have friendzone men that don't have what you need or stop talking to them all together. I was not going to be "Boo Boo the Fool" hanging around a man who bad mouth me or didn't act like they wanted me. The last man that did that ended up losing me, and a year later, I was dating the man I would marry.

    I was not afraid to Let Him GO! If he is reading this, he knows. You gotta let people know you are worth the long haul and you are in it - to win it. Glenn and I both connected physically, but I didn't see that part first, although I am sure he did. He got a thing for dark skin

Release Your Passion - Enjoy Sex

women, full body, and not afraid to speak on it.

He grew up in a house with a single mother and his brothers, and he was never rude, distasteful, or less than a gentleman - his mother taught him that. We don't become belligerent or angry with each other, but we will raise our voice, especially when we–well you know. But we have an understanding. I will not call you out your name, and you won't call me out my name. We have never had this problem in our marriage or relationship in all the 29 years we have known each other.

We have mutual respect, and that was what worked for us first. He was a gentleman, and we became good friends. We are really a pair of nerds who have a freaky side we both like. We both weren't shy about what we wanted and what we liked. If you can't talk to your spouse in a blunt, straight-to-the-point way, you need to get over that right now. Because it doesn't make sense to be in a relationship forever and you can't get what you need.

We tested the waters before we got married. As you know, we had our first daughter before we got married. I knew before buying the car that I wanted it, and he did, too. I don't think we ever thought we wouldn't be together, but we didn't get married because of our baby. We got married because we worked together, loved each other, and wanted to keep working together. Marriage is a partnership, so you both have to take ownership of what you want.

My husband clearly understood the assignment when it came to me. I love this man because there is a lot I don't have to say. He got it, and his spontaneous nature keeps me wanting it, and it ain't never got old.

For people out there having dry, old, raggedy sex, I feel so bad for you because it doesn't have to be that way! Y'all need to talk and get some things on the table. You need to establish some ground rules because there are things I am not ever doing.

He got things he is not ever gonna do. We got the deal breakers down in the beginning. When you have an open and honest conversation about sex, attraction, and what you want out of a relationship, you free yourselves to enjoy it. You can be free to explore each other, laugh, touch, joke, and play. There is nothing better than being able to get sexually ravaged by your husband. Ohhh lord, have mercy. He can have you speaking in tongues! Yes, I am speaking from experience!!

This is a grown-woman book, so if you don't know where I am coming from, skip the chapter and carry on. For you ladies, please find that spark in your marriage and have the conversations very directly. Ask questions like, "What turns you on?" Then let him talk. Listen to the man, and then it is your turn to speak and do the same thing, answer with honesty, or you will be miserable and pay for it.

Nobody is a mind reader. He doesn't know what you like or what you want if you don't say anything. This is not the only question you should ask, this should be the first question. Girl, you gotta get in there. You need to ask him, "What position or positions do you like?" "Do you want a tongue or not? Can I touch you here or how do you feel about this?" Ask the questions you shouldn't be asking nobody else. This is your husband, not a fly by the night booty call. Enjoy yourself.

Don't be afraid to throw some roadblocks up in the day, either. Wear something sexy while you are cooking dinner, and you might get some before the dinner finishes. Hell, you might have dinner and dessert that night! Men are simple, and they want us to want it just as much as they do. Most men are ready before you ask, but if you initiate it girl, you might see another side of standing to attention you ain't never seen!

Our trip to Tanzania for my 50th birthday celebration still got me hollerin', okay. Listen to this: I had the most amazing orgasm of my life. So, I am telling you, gotta have fun and keep things fresh and spicy. Don't try to be so rigid and put things on a schedule. If you are in the mood feeling hot and bothered, girl, you better go jump his bones.

If you do it, you give no other woman a chance to even step in your territory. Now, I don't say that to mean you are comparing yourself or competing with other women. Listen, remember this is your husband, so you make sure he knows you want him at all times!!

BUT, make no mistake about it. I know Glenn knows what I am putting down, and before he would ever think about doing something stupid, all our good times would flood his mind and remind him clearly who I am. This is why I wish a woman would.

Melvina W.

We live in Atlanta, and the disrespect someone has is atrocious. I don't mind when they stare and look like they are trying to eat him with their eyes. I know what I got. Why do you think I married him?

If you know what you got, don't be afraid to ask for it. I joke around sometimes and even beg for it, and girl, he loves it! Men want to be desired, too. They have something to offer us, too.

I am a woman, a wife, a business owner, a friend, and all that other stuff, but I got a vagina too! She has demands and needs, and I am gonna speak up for her just like I do everything else. I ain't never scared to say what I want, and yes, I get it here too!

My husband takes really good care of me. He looks out for me by getting me things I don't ask for. It is not uncommon for him to buy me food and ensure I eat because he knows I am not leaving the computer on some nights.

He buys me diamonds, which are my best friends. We can go out together and we both got money. I am shopping, and he knows I am going to bash an eye or show a little leg to get him to say yes to something I want.

I pay him back in "coochie coupons" because we have an understanding. What keeps me attracted to him is the fact that he is always asking and pursuing me for sex. He treats me like a QUEEN and knows how to run in between the sheets! He is always complimenting me and bringing me flowers, gold, diamonds and all.

Release Your Passion - Enjoy Sex

It feels like my birthday four or five times a week. He follows me around and literally "screws" me hard like he has never had sex before. Girl, if I could tell you how many orgasms I get in a week, I need the off days to sleep! Geesh!!! It is getting hot here!! Yes, ladies, I recommend you Let It Go and enjoy the incredible orgasms!

I ask Glenn, what makes you like this? What do you love about me? He tells me he has always loved my dark skin, first and foremost. Then my butt. Yes, this flat-dimpled-up butt he loves (though I don't know why) and my personality. He has always told me he likes my personality. I enjoy laughing with my husband and just being myself. I am bossy, sassy, and I say what I want, and he loves it. It takes a strong man to be able to handle me, and he has made me tap out too many times! I am a blessed woman, and I know it.

But I wanted to write this chapter for you to help you release your passion in your relationship. So let me tell you a few pointers from my point of view that can help some of you out. I jump straight in on sex because with a husband like mine, it is always on your mind. Yes, I get my work done, but I still can look at him from the corner of my eye, and if he is naked, I'm taking a break!

But for you young in love couples, you might not be at this stage yet. For those of you getting back to dating or wanting to give love and marriage another shot, here are some things that helped me. Love is about fully understanding that love has to be exposed by giving yourself freely to that person by way of com-

Melvina W.

municating about everything and agreeing to disagree. Love is first built in a relationship. You have to be able to communicate and speak freely.

Love is not fear of what someone will think, feel, or say. Love should allow you to speak about anything and not worry about an outcome but to be open about the journey. Love is a journey you both are on together. You are getting to know each other, and you should allow one another to be free and feel the butterflies. Glenn and I are in our fifties, but we both get those giddy high school vibes still for one another. These are some of the ways you know you married the right person.

They help you to feel young and just love life. When you go through hard times, because they are gonna come, you want someone who can love you through the changes. You don't want someone who makes you feel judged, put down, low, or brings down your self-esteem. You want someone that can be on your team and you can be on theirs.

Marriage is not for the weak. Yes, you will have hard conversations, but you must stay committed to communicating. When you stop talking, you can kiss the relationship goodbye. Two people who don't talk can't find common ground. They cannot find peace, happiness, or joy in that. This is a recipe for divorce or infidelity, which neither you want in your marriage. You have to marry someone you can talk to.

I was married once before my husband, and that marriage was a mistake. We couldn't talk. We argued and fought all the time. I was young when I got married, so there was a whole lot I didn't know, but I learned in good timing before meeting and marrying Glenn. It took some time for me to grow up and know what I wanted in a husband. When I found it in him, it was like white on rice when I jumped on marrying him.

We didn't have a big wedding or anything like that. We did a courthouse wedding and saved all that money. This is something I would change a little bit because I got married once before at the courthouse with my first husband. I might have a wedding in the future. We will see if it means that much to Glenn or my father. I know my father would want to walk me down the aisle, too, because he didn't get a chance to do that either. Hmmm, maybe one day?

I am about experiences and doing what makes us happy. You have to have tunnel vision between you and your spouse. Although you can appreciate other people's thoughts and feedback, what you and your husband discuss is what should be law. Please leave others and all family members out of your marriage, and make sure you truly listen to each other!
You have to protect your marriage from the ideas and judgment of others. No one knows better than you about what you need to do to make it.

Love is a crucial part of having great sex. Sex without love is nothing but just sex - UNTIL or WHEN you fall in love. When you are comfortable, and you both have an understanding of each other, sex is phenomenal. Sex has always been front and center in our relationship because I live with a man who doesn't want to go too long without sex. He knows how to break up my day and help me take much-needed breaks from coding or whatever I have going on. For us, sex is a stress reliever, and if you have NO money and all you can do is stay in the house, sex is your best friend.

Yes, on those rough nights when you lose your job or something happens and we are stuck in the house, good night, children. "But Mom, it is only 6:30." I know the sun is going down somewhere, so why not take a nap or something or enjoy a bit of tv in your room?" I say that as I close the door. Glenn follows right behind me. We knew how to enjoy every high and low of our lives together.

Now, men and women are different. For him, sex fixes things, but for me, I might be so busy and focused sex is not on my mind. If we have deadlines and things to get done, I might have to hold out a day or two, and he will let me. But I will pay for it on day three, and I lick my lips as I wait for the day. There is NOT enough ice water in my jug to replenish the water I lose messing around with Glenn. But for a man, the lights can be turned off for nonpayment, and he will think it is an invitation to have sex. Never mind, the lights are off, and we have an issue here.

If a man is neglecting his other duties and is only alive for the sex part, it can make a woman feel used and belittled. You may want to lash out or withhold sex if you feel like you are being used because things you need are not being done. This is where conversations go a long way. If you need him to do something for you, don't be shy about what you need to feel

Release Your Passion - Enjoy Sex
sexy and in the mood.

Seeing my husband take care of business is really sexy to me. Sometimes, it is not about clothes, hot showers, and things like that. It is about his consistency and willingness to make my day easier, that I like. I voice that to him, and he delivers. You have to tell the man what you need and want so he can meet your demands or do what women should do: use their power tools.

I am not saying take advantage of the man to get your way. I am saying this: I know he wants it, so I have a list of things I want to do-- and he hears best when he wants to have sex. So before that conversation, we had my conversation. I want compliments, flowers, gold, and diamonds. Also, I want him to pay bills and help me clean up the house. I expect him to be respectful at all times because I do the same. I have a list that goes on and on, but as he meets my list, I rise to the occasion for what he wants from me. I am not the only one having fun; he is having fun as well. But he is going to have to work for the poo-nanny over here!!!

Yes, most women know that "our goods" will have a man do all kinds of things. There are women who weaponize it for their own gain, and they don't care about the man. And the men know it is true also. Some guys use their ding dongs in the same way as leverage. Most men know to buy gifts, come to family outings, and do things the woman is asking for so they can get some of these "warm cookies"!

Melvina W.

I don't see anything wrong with people setting standards or things they want for men to get some. I feel like if you don't want to pay the price, you will move on, and vice versa. If you are not getting what you want sexually or enjoying your sex life, you need to better communicate. Closed mouths don't get fed.

Also, don't be so stuffy with sex. Sex was meant to be fun and enjoyable. Relax. Go out and explore other things in the sexual arena. Maybe buy toys, look at the internet or porn to get some ideas of new things you can try. Communicate on what you want to be done to your body and let him work it out.

I ain't never scared to try something new with Glenn, and the best sex is sex away from home! I told you when I went to Tanzania, it was like a lion came out of him that he didn't have at home. He was wild and free and my body was enjoying every moment of it. I remember the grabs, the sweat, and the heartbeats we had that felt like African music playing in the background. I could not stop, and we screwed like jackrabbits all day and night-- in our 50's, I might add!

You would have thought the time I blew my back out it was because Glenn and I had a wild night. I had so many friends give me the side eye because I hurt my back. But no, it wasn't from being with Glenn, and it didn't stop me from getting down, either. I just had to be careful, hahaha. We work through the challenges, and we make sure to have a physical connection.

When we went to Columbia, South America, for New Year's one year, Glenn had hurt his arm just before the flight. We were concerned about how things would go on the trip. I wanted to be sympathetic, but I also wanted the sex I loved away from home. Girl, there wasn't a dry moment on this trip. We did a dang thing, you hear me! And I checked every part of him to make sure he was working to full capacity–and he was.

I remember one time when we were messing around, and I was trying to see what we were going to do. I asked him as we exchanged a few wet, passionate kisses, "Hey, let's try the slip-and-slide situation, do you mind? Want to try it with me?"

He almost bolted into action to get naked, and he replied, "Ohhh, okay, sure!!" Before I could catch my breath, my sweetie pie got the oil all over the bed and was slipping and sliding trying to slip things in and all. We were sliding all over the bed, and the orgasm was epic.

I enjoy my relationship with Glenn and I don't mind sharing some details, you know. I know the older generation, like my parents, probably don't talk as openly as I do about sex. But couples my age and younger are not shy about speaking about sex.

I think this is good and healthy. Depending on a person's upbringing, it can be hard to be open about sex. I know that Glenn and I talk about what we want loud and clear. I am very open and will talk about sex with anyone, but Glenn is more discrete and will ONLY talk with me!!

However, if talking is hard for you, there are

other things you can do to communicate what you like. You can write letters, send notes, emails, and sex text with emojis if images are too much. Phone sex is great sex when you are not near each other, and one of you gets horny. When I worked away from home, we had to make that work for several months while I was working out of town. Man those nights had me drooling when I got back home, just thinking about the night we would have.

I firmly believe in sex with marriage, and I firmly believe in women withholding themselves for several months to make sure he is worthy of you. I firmly believe in being in a monogamous relationship before even having sex with a man. I firmly believe that whatever my husband wants me to do to get him off or hot in the sexual arena, I will do; he is my husband! I firmly believe in making it clear to him what I want in the bedroom because, as women, we are the ones who have to be warmed to get things going.

We are NOT wired like men to drop our clothes and say we are ready, nooooo!!! But if you do NOT teach a man how or where or what you want in the bedroom, they will be oblivious and keep doing what they have been doing. Let's face it: it doesn't take much to get them off.

I treat my kitty cat like gold and diamonds. It is precious; I firmly believe that women should not spread their legs and give it to any man just because he asked, looks good, or whatever! I think and love me much more than that. I strenuously encourage love and being in love and having sex with one person in a long-term

Release Your Passion - Enjoy Sex

committed relationship, preferably your husband!

If you are at a point where having sex with your husband gets hard. Or the other person is not open to speaking with you about sext. You can try to be patient and thoughtful in how you communicate. Try to play with them, kiss them, nibble on their ear, and do little things to help lighten the mood. Don't make it feel like a reprimand.

You two are in a relationship and likely married. You want to be mindful of how you speak to each other and consider each other's feelings. Not everyone will want or like the same things. It is okay if you don't. Try to be open and honest about how you feel and consider each other as you communicate.

Sex is something that is a vital part of a marriage to me. This is part of the bonding between husband and wife; you should enjoy this experience. If you start to separate in the bedroom, you want to see what was the root cause for the separation. Usually, it is not even sex but other situations that might steal the desire to be intimate with each other.

Don't allow things to creep up in your marriage, and you do not address it. Don't allow others to have a large say about your marriage and risk running off your spouse or chasing off their desire. Don't let the flame die, although at times, it can fade or flicker. It is normal to have some separation here and there.

Glenn and I had a few moments that were very difficult for us, and I had to turn down jobs because it was too taxing on my marriage and our relationship. If you have a schedule of three to four times a week, you have to keep that. Nothing should break your bond in that sense for long extended periods because that means one of you will be lacking. Occasional changes are expected, but if this is a need and it is not being met, it can cause problems. Adjust and work to make the changes a marriage requires.

I do want to say that even if Glenn and I reached a point where we could not have sex anymore, I would not leave him. I have always been about more than that for him. I want a relationship with him whether we have sex or not if that makes sense. I mean, I love sex, but it is a bonus that I enjoy. BUT if Glenn can not have sex with me anymore, we will still be married, and I would love him the same.

I love every moment we share together, and I certainly won't forget it. It is not a deal breaker for me if we don't have sex, and I don't believe it is for him, either. We are committed to each other through thick or thin. Our sexual journey has increased our relationship for sure, but it is not the foundation of our love. We will never forget to let go of the things that don't matter so we can protect what does matter.

Moving on.

26 YEARS MARRIED

Let Go of Judgment

I have been telling you to let a lot of stuff go because it isn't helping you. One area of our lives that we all can struggle with is how we see ourselves. It is easy to think that we got it all together but it is hard to hide what we really feel when we compare ourselves to others.

I will happily compare myself to other people all day long because this is how you see where you are and what you might need to work on. If I am afraid to look at what I have going on, how am I going to find my flaws–if I had them? How will I see what I am good at and know more about what I am bringing to the table? Most importantly, how will I know what direction I want to move into if I don't have a roadmap?

I have a roadmap that I created for medical coding and a mentorship program to help new or experienced coders. One of the key fundamentals I have learned is when you are learning something new or trying to get into a new business or career, you will need someone to point you to your north. You will need a guide, roadmap, mentor, or a figure you look up to so you can see what they have to help you know what you want.

I watch people all day. If I want to know quickly if I am listening to you or if I will compare myself to you, you have to have something going on that I want. You have to do something that I don't do, or I want to learn. You can offer a product or service that when I compare it to what I got going on, I clearly know that I need you.

If the same rules were to be applied to me, I would expect people to look at what I do for a living. I would expect medical coders to see if I got a bank account, experience, and a success rate that points to what they want to achieve. If you look at my career to compare what you have been doing with yours, you are going to get way more positive solutions for your life than negative.

I am a very positive person. I have a strong mindset to succeed and help others do the same. I do have a giving heart, but I am not a sucker for love or

Let Go of Judgment

a creature of bad habit. If something isn't working for me, I am the first to let it go, no matter what it is.

If you look at my marriage, my children, and how I think, you should compare yourself to what I am doing so you can get a gauge for what you have been doing. This is not to beat yourself up, but it will challenge you to seek out what you really want. If you don't know what you want in your life right now, look at what people have in life and compare apples to apples. Sometimes you are comparing oranges to apples and you need to know that is the case.

I am not on everyone's level and many are not on mine. I don't try to pretend or give excuses for why my life is or isn't going in the direction I want. I look for solutions. Having a solution-driven mindset is paramount if you want to change your life, and yes, I believe that means opening your eyes and looking around you. You need to be aware of what's going on so you can be encouraged and see what your life could be like.

There is such a thing as healthy comparison. A healthy comparison will light a fire underneath and point to areas of your life where you can improve. I will be the first to say I am learning.

Although I have everything I do, and I have done all that I have done, there is always something for me to improve upon. You can compare people when you are looking at them, services, or what you want. I do recognize stereotypes because they didn't get there by accident - trust me, it is some fact to it.

Melvina W.

Stereotypes can be negative, but I choose not to allow that to be the case. I have a positive and balanced approach to comparison. When people break out of the mold, that is what can make them look at them more and wonder. I admire people for all kinds of things. Money is the biggest, but I watch what people accomplish and compare that to me to see what I need to do next in my life.

With all that said, I don't believe in negative comparisons. I believe in comparing to help you step up your game and get better. The way you can avoid the pitfall of negatively comparing yourself and others, you need to focus on being honest with yourself. Denial will only delay what you could be working on. If you say there is nothing wrong with me over here, but you have a family history of problems that you know of, be humble and look at it again.

If you find that other people are trying to tell you something about yourself and you got blinders on to not see it, I would say wake up and see if there is any truth in it. I know looking at things that point to us not having it all together can hurt our feelings and make us think negatively. Remember, that is not the intent to beat you up with comparison. It is not meant to drive jealousy and separation–unless you need to let it go and move on.

You have to know yourself and what you are working on so you can avoid comparison for no good reason. It is easy to tell people or yourself, "I am no good." I never use negative self-talk in my comparison. If I am not good at something and I see it, I don't make

Let Go of Judgment

negative comments. I say positive reinforcement comments that help me to face the facts but also create a healthy disposition to make changes.

I know who I am, considering the good and the bad about me. I am good at medical coding, but I am not the greatest at losing weight. I am great at expressing my feelings and what I want, so I lean on my strong suit as I move through new ideas to build the confidence to keep going. I don't make excuses that I cannot do something because I am not doing something.

I hear people tell me, "I know Melvina, you can do this because you are YOU. I am not you, and I cannot do this like you do." When you make comments like that, you are negatively comparing yourself.

You don't always realize it, but when you compare and draw a negative conclusion, like I can't because I can't, there is nowhere to go. You don't want to pigeonhole yourself into a negative headspace. Try looking for ways to say yes, I can do something instead of no, I can't, and here is why.

Why? Because negative self-talk brings you down and doesn't build you up. Or, it can create a negative relationship within your mind for change and growth. You don't want to hate your way into growth. You want to find encouraging and healthy reasons to make changes in your life that will make you a better person. I know my ability.

If right now I had to change my life and go in a different direction because what I was doing stopped working, I know where to look. I would first focus on what was important and take the steps one at a time. What I would not do, is be out here holding my freaking hand out, expecting someone to do it for me. People need to get bold, get confidence, and know they can do what they see others do. It could take money, time, resources, and patience for some of us.

If you want anything bad enough, none of this will scare you off. If you are saying you want it, why are you sitting around waiting, begging, and crying? Why are you saying nobody wants to help me get this together or do that?

What the hell is this? You don't wait around and see what others want to give you; you go for what you need in life and take it! You have to be hungry and ready to eat to get the food you need, not make excuses to feel sorry for yourself and have a pity party.

Focus on what you want and not what others want for you or are telling you what to do. YOU don't compare yourself to get others to tell you what to do. You focus on what others are doing to show you how to do what you want to do. You need to check in with yourself.

Here I am, half deaf. You think I didn't have to reassess constantly when most jobs rely on your hearing? Most jobs expect you to hear directions and follow them, problem for me: What if I cannot hear you?

There are aids to help with this, but that doesn't mean I may receive and understand information the

Let Go of Judgment

same as others who can lean on abilities I don't have. I have to find my strengths and weaknesses in all areas so I can find a way through it. I need to be able to keep a job to pay my bills, so I need to know in what environments I can win. If there is an office setting where people are quiet, in the office, and you have to whisper to get things done, I won't fit in there.

I know that I am loud. I like working in my zone, playing music sometimes, and being me. If that disrupts the atmosphere, I compare what they have going on to what I have at home. I like what I do better, and I am more efficient. When you compare, it is not to change everything about you to look like someone else. Some things won't work for you and you will have to change it up or don't do it altogether.

I know my challenges and limitations like I know my gifts. Having a job serving people standing on my feet is also something I am not going to do. I am fifty-plus years old. What the hell do I look like doing that? I am not built for that, and if you aren't built for stuff either, find a way to make it happen.

Sit down and make a vision board to plan your life. Sit down and play jazz music and see what you like, who you are, and what you are doing. Make bullet points to get some of these answers. Make a pros and cons list, and also look for the things you like. If I was to make a bullet list, it would look like this:

Who am I:
I am a mother
A wife

Melvina W.

A black woman
A medical coder
A Sorority Sister
A business owner
A author
A mentor
A coach

I know what I love:
Family
Money
Medical Coding
Making Money
Having Money
Having opportunities

I know my negatives:
I can be highly sarcastic
Very abrasive
Very direct
Some don't care, and I don't care they don't care.

I am not careless, but I don't care about everyone's opinions. Expectations are important and stereotypes are what pushed me out of my comfort zone. I remember when I had no degrees, yes, sitting up in the house on the homeboy network with a baby on the way.

I was a stereotype that started this way, and the world would have been okay with me staying this way. Amounting to a person who is okay with what I have and not striving to make more than 80k a year. For some of us, that is all we hope for.

Let Go of Judgment

Some people can feel anything more is unrealistic and that you should agree with them. What they don't tell you is that in that boat, it is sinking. So when you jump on board, you are going down and watching others rise above you, who got it right. Those who decided they were not accepting less, those who wanted more, rose above 80k, which is now way back in their rearview mirror. People who can overcome a stereotype get kudos from me because I know what it took me to do it.

I won't be sitting in a sinking boat. I am not like them. Like that song I love to listen to, "There Not Like Us." I stand on that, and I won't drop down to meet others' expectations. A lot of people around me are Christians. I am not a Christian, so there is no reason to put me in that bracket. There are things I am not, and I don't want you to put me in that category.

There is an expectation that all black people are to vote Democrat. I am not a Democrat, and I don't vote blue. There, I said it. I got a lot of bad vibes, negative flak, and lost friends from my political views.

I don't care. I know what I need and what my convictions are, and other people's expectations of that or of me is something they can fight with if they want to or let me go! I didn't vote for our former Vice President Kamala Harris and voted instead for Donald J. Trump. I have no regrets about it at all. People expect and look at us to be grouped together when we are not the same.

I am not living my life to please everyone or anybody. I am not in pain if people don't like me or appreciate what I am putting down. I would like for people to see it of course, but I am not going to be heartbroken if you don't. No, this is not going to make me do something I don't want to do. This does not bring out my emotions or make me emotional.

It just makes me think, "Got damn, how long are YOU going to be emotional about this?" If you must be emotional, sure, but be reasonable. Be emotional for a few minutes and channel the energy to something that will work for you. Make it positive to make it happen for you. Live to see another day and know they will be alright and you too.

Give yourself a pep talk. If people are not on the same train you are on, keep it moving. Nine times out of ten, they are not going to shop where I shop. They are not going to go where I go.

They are not my audience; my job isn't to win everybody but those I intentionally make it my job to capture. I don't have to get all the money, even though I want to, hahaha. My goal is not to leave any of my money on the table.

I want what is mine, and I am going to get it come hell or high water. You already know how I do. So, if people are not on my level, I know how to get on. I know how to believe for better and find it. I am not staying on a job where I know I could have more.

I believe in having my medical coding school because I show people how to get more out of life using what I did that works. The proof is in the pudding! So,

Let Go of Judgment

what is in your pudding again? Do you have some sugar and milk, or is your pudding still just the powder that is all dried up? Only you would know, hmmm?

I am building generational wealth. So, if people are not doing that, they are not my audience, and I will get out of the conversation so quickly. Knowing this is my rock and helps me to transition my life. Talks like this make me more confident in being who I am.

I remember being at a Christmas party last year and hearing a woman ask the question or make the statement that motivational books don't work. She essentially said, "I don't understand motivation and feel good about yourself books because, let's say you can do 1, 2 and 3, that doesn't mean you are going to get out of your situation. So they really don't work." I said, "Really? They don't work? It works for me, so you saying it can't work for anyone else?"

Then she had the excuse, "That's you, Melvina." Girl, I am half-deaf, black, overweight, and have every tick in the book for why people could tell me no. The difference, I don't accept it. I am going to tell you that if you pay to come to my medical coding school, allow me to mentor you, and show you the ropes, I can get you there.

I didn't say it would be easy, but I CAN do it. I have been doing it for countless coders already. "This is a system already in motion, and it works." There is proof in my pudding, some whipped cream on top and even a cherry!!

Melvina W.

She replied with how she doesn't have food or gas money week after week and I instantly thought, "What the hell are you doing with your money?" I told her she needed to find the money. If you want to invest in something and you need fifty dollars a week to do it, and you can't, there is a fundamental problem here.

The problem isn't the money because no matter what the dollar amount is, she would have an excuse. The issue is that she is not disciplined in her life to find the money. She is not focused enough on her true goal and so the excuses rise up to fit the occasion.

I say I want to publish my books. I didn't say whew, that is going to be expensive. I didn't complain about the price and try to haggle prices either. I reached into my account and paid it because this is for me.

If I want it, I will work for it. I will find the money to get what I want. I will be disciplined and tell myself no over there if that means I get what I want right here.

She said when she got the fifty dollars she had to ditch it out on bills before she could pay for her investment. I said, I will wash cars before I go to bed that night to make the money. I will clean up houses or do whatever to get them few dollars. Twenty, fifty, or even one hundred dollars is NOT much, and as the prices increase, I now say the same thing because I have a mentality that defies the amount. I will find a way to get that money that day, and the day won't end until I find it. The difference between me and you is that I am hungry and willing to go do what I need to do to make

Let Go of Judgment
it out on the other side.

So I asked her, "What do you think makes me so much different than you?" We both are black women, come from humble backgrounds, are married, and say we want something out of life. What did she think this is?

That I am high on the hog and can't relate to where she is at? She only could reply with the same thing, "That's you, Melvina." She is clearly not ready and NOT picking up what I am putting down. She does not believe in seeing the forest beyond the trees, believes there is gold at the end of the rainbow, or believes in infinite possibilities.

How can you and your husband not get twenty, fifty, or even one hundred dollars combined? You got help! There are single mothers out here making ways out of no way. They are hustling, and many of them are doing fine. They've learned to adjust.

The same way she does not believe in infinite possibilities is the same way I stabilize myself. I am always confident. I am on this throne, and I am not coming down from it. Because if I fail, it is not because I was playing ball on your terms in your court, it will be on my own dime and time, not yours. Seeing her lack of belief makes me even more of a believer because I am who I am, and this motivates me even more!

So this is why I make decisions others don't. I don't care when people compare themselves with me, and what they got isn't what I want. I don't feel guilty about not listening to others, and when people try to say that is you, Melvina. I live up to MY expectations. If I fail today and I am outside collecting cans, it is because I want to. At the same time, if I make ten million dollars and want to buy a house by a celebrity it is because I did it and want to.

Listen to this: I have a homegirl/friend from Savannah, Georgia. We have known each other for over 40 plus years due to the fact that our families both attended the same church. Monica and I reconnected in Jacksonville, Florida, when I relocated from Lithonia for a medical coding job at Mayo Clinic in 2007.

Funny story: I was talking to someone telling them that I am from Savannah, Georgia, and she walked by overhearing me because, as usual I am loud due to my hearing loss. I will never forget she said you are from Savannah, and I was like, yes…and the rest is herstory!!

From 2007 to 2011, I lived in Jacksonville, Florida with my family. These were times when I had NOT started my business and was literally a medical coder who was fairly new to the industry. I bought a house in Lithonia, and please remember that I was "supposed" to be renting my house out, but that was very unsuccessful! While living in Jacksonville FL, we still had to pay bills back at home, too.

So, I have a mortgage and rent to pay every month, married, three kids, electricity, water, gas, car insurance, and more to pay every month. Listen, pulling in like about 125K with both of us was NOT enough money for me. We just did not have enough money, pretty much!

Now, here is Monica, she is seeing my lights turn off. She is witnessing of my financial struggle to make more happen. I was always bitchin' and having a moment because I knew I was better than how I was living. I didn't get a job, and our problems went away. It was hard work for all of us to adjust and deal with not making enough. I knew I had to do better than this was my thought process.

Monica's situation is one far left from mine: trust and believe. She is a single mother with three sons. Her struggle is far worse; she was living beyond paycheck to paycheck, and she was counting on income tax refunds to pay rent, car, and all. She had worked several low-paying jobs to try to survive and make ends meet. She's had several horrific relationships during survival mode that thankfully ended for the best.

Monica struggled to continue by living in her car with her three children, going without food, and things continuously getting turned off. When she said the struggle was real, she meant REALLY struggling with her family. Considering she was my friend and homegirl, she had some assistance from me for food, gas money, and even shelter at times.

However, she did manage to graduate from college with her Associates degree. She kept fighting for better circumstances for her and her kids. She always knew there was a better life or she needed to have a better life or circumstance than what she had ever had previously.

Monica was looking at my life and saw a better setup. Even though, in my eyes, it wasn't a perfect setup to me. But to Monica, she saw a better future through me and my life.

Throughout the years, we have stayed in touch and saw each other from time to time. However, I denied Monica my medical coding school training, and the reason being I felt she was NOT ready because of her circumstances. I looked at her life and saw so many obstacles; therefore I felt she was NOT ready at all for the medical coding world.

But through the years, we tried the medical coding training later in 2017 and it caused us to have a major fallout. That caused a seven-year hiatus of no communication, with the door still open a little if either person wanted to reconcile the relationship. Why the hiatus?

As you all know, I am a very strong-willed, business-minded, and extremely cut-throat type of person with my business and in the world of medical coding. Monica was very compassionate and not ready to receive me in that type of setting, which is in my business world. She saw friend Melvina, not business Melvina.

Basically, we are both females. One more emotional than the other, words were said that were true… but Melvina decided to Let It Go. That meant letting Monica go because I felt that it was too difficult and

Let Go of Judgment

that there was no reason to hold onto her with the drama or negative feelings that were displayed.

You must know that Monica, back then from 2007 to 2017, had a different mindset. When she reached out, she had a major mindset change and came to realize several positive outlooks on life. Whereas I had the same mindset, I just escalated and grew even more over the years.

My train was still moving and was NOT slowing down. She did NOT value herself or believe that the forest was beyond the trees like I did! Due to the situational life happenings, we were on opposite ends of the map!

She saw this and knew, "Houston, we have a problem." She was still doing the same thing, wanting a different result, and I pointed that out to her. She knew it was something wrong - I knew something was right over here and still moving forward no matter what. I tried to help.

How we reconnected: Now, let's fast forward to November 2024, Monica has been reaching out through the years via messaging me. I was ignoring those messages again because I had Let It Go. BUT BUT you MUST understand, by the grace of GOD, I responded to her on November 19th, 2024 ....and we reconnected.

Why? To be honest with you, I have always loved Monica and her three boys and cared for them. I probably understood her better than she understood herself, and basically, that evening, I just said what the

Melvina W.

hell, why not?

I knew I ignored her repeatedly over the years, and I knew why. She was probably in the same situation as before. Maybe now, I had a heart to try to help again although I didn't know it yet. I just opened the door more and let my heart respond. That is my answer! So why NOT sooner, you may ask? It is my defense mechanism. I was hurt by the things she said in 2017.

I was disappointed because I tried, and I stated that it wasn't going to work out. I went against my better judgment. I convinced myself that I did not need her and that I could do whatever I could on my own without her in my life.

Enrollment details and Progress in the course: OMG, in terms of helping her now. I wanted to show her how she can get GOLD at the end of the rainbow!! I did need her as my friend / homegirl this whole time, though I survived.

I am glad we reconnected, even though it took seven years. I am fortunate that we are still living, and it was NOT too late! About my dear Monica …she is down-to-earth and funny! She is actually motivating and inspiring me that I can, and I will mentor even more!

She has become another success story to this day for my medical coding school, Infinity HIM Medical Coding School! In November, she dropped the money to enroll in my medical coding school, consulting, and mentoring program. She came to slay and was NOT

Let Go of Judgment
playing!

Unlike before, we both could have an honest and open conversation and see each other's position. I wanted her to believe in herself, and she needed me to mentor her. I needed more patience and time.

Understand this, she reached out and stated that she was ready. Come hell or high water. She is finishing my course after listening to my podcast! In December, before the eight weeks, she was finished with the school, asking what is next. Her progression with the course was phenomenal and with urgency like she was hungry and never have eaten before in her life!

How did she stay motivated to finish? Because when I accepted her once again. Monica did not take the opportunity lightly. She knew that NOW was HER time in her life to make a difference with a different mindset, outlook and growth. She put on her big girl's drawers!! It was TIME she said! So, why me? Why do you think Monica came back or even tried to connect with me?

Monica has stated that in her circle, she does not have anyone making boss moves. And Monica witnessed firsthand throughout the years how I went ALL THE WAY UP!! And her circumstances stayed the same and I was advancing as I always do! It was a NO-brainer once Monica made up her mind that it was time for a change who to go to: Me, Melvina!

Results and Future Ahead: With Monica the proof is in the pudding, she has passed the Certified Professional Coder (CPC) and the Certified Risk Coder Certifications (CRC). She is actively training exclusively with me to learn different specialties. Along with interviewing skills, resume writing, and more!! The future is here.

She is making boss moves, buying a house, making six figures, investing, launching another business, perhaps! The sky is the limit with her, especially since we have reconnected and are going all the way up as friends and with our mentor/mentee relationship!! She got back on Melvina's train, and I am helping her get to where she wants to go!!

Testimony - it works the only thing that stops it is YOU and your mindset!! She is living proof! That it can work, and it will work, for sure!! From November 2024 to February 2025, she started the program, completed it, took the exams, and passed with the help of Infinity HIM School. She did this all while working a full-time job with NO excuses!

And she is a believer!! No doubts, no questions that this works. She will tell you that if you NEED to change your life, you need to have faith! Step out on faith and make it happen, Come Hell or High Water.

Let Go of Judgment

Keep up with me because she Didn't say it Was Over - she has only started to live!!

So, if you are feeling guilty when others throw their monkey wrench of life into your show, there is a disconnect. If you feel bad because you are not meeting other people's expectations and those don't align with your goals, there is a problem. The problem shouldn't be with you because you have to live your life like they do. She went home with the excuse I can't find twenty dollars. And I went home with the money in my account, the nice house I love, and the husband that will screw me silly.

I love my life, and I know that not everybody has my story. I am happy, and I make no apologies for it. I am free! I am not doing anything I don't want to do, and if I have to do something I don't like for a season, it is going to be for a big reason. I see that as part of what I want or need, so I endure. I know that nothing lasts forever; life is fluid, and it moves.

Knowing that time has to move on does mean I have to guard what I focus on. It is not that I don't care about other people because I do. I could list things I do, but I do them not to be acknowledged but because I want a legacy, and it does my heart good to help people. So, it's not that I don't care about people like some may think after reading a bit of what I said so far. Keep this in mind: I love people. I just love me more.

So, I do want to be clear: when I say cut people off or take your distance, don't allow people to put you in a box. I would be sad if they were in a box. I would

Melvina W.

mourn the death of those past. I will probably come to the funeral. However, I am not going to stop my life because someone else's life stopped. I mean that if they stop moving in life, stop breathing, or just stop wanting more in life. I will not stick around for that.

Like anything, I think morning should be for a time, but you cannot let your life fall apart in the meantime. This doesn't make you callous or insensitive but points to what is important for you. Why do people feel they need to beg others to allow them to love themselves and spend time on what they care about?

We are here on earth to live our lives both individually and with others. You have to balance the two, and you spend most of your time alone. You are born alone, and you will die alone. This means you are not the world around you when you stop breathing.

To be transparent, it was hard when I saw my brother struggling with life. He chose a very different path from mine. Unfortunately, some of those choices could have led to him not being here. He passed away several years back, and I still grieve his loss from time to time. I do miss him, but I couldn't go down the rabbit hole with him. When he was making his decisions for how he wanted to live or smoke up his life, I had to respect that.

I respect my husband and my daughters, too, but I will call a spade a spade. I told my brother what I saw and how I felt he could do better, and I meant that. My mindset is to speak what I see to be helpful and loving. I don't think love means no judgment. In fact, I think it

Let Go of Judgment
is the opposite.

I think it is funny when people tell me, "Melvina, you shouldn't judge." I do it all the time, and that won't change. Maybe it's my commentary because I don't always share my thoughts but I do say at least to myself, "We are not doing that."

You need boundaries to protect yourself, and I fully enforce mine. If I am not where I want to be, I put something in place to get there. If you don't have what you need in life, you need to silence the noise and enforce your boundaries. When you see the gold at the end of the tunnel, it will encourage you to move towards it. You need to make less time for BS and keep going no matter what.

I can be one of the most inviting people you EVER could meet. The question is, will you stay inside my world? Many people tell me I should mentor, but not everyone will fit into my unit.

Money helps, but friendships don't last if I don't think people make the cut. I can work with you but not keep you in my inner circle. We meet people for different reasons, so make sure you know why you are connecting with people.

It should be mutual for the friends you make. I love being a giver and to mutual exchange information, but I don't want to be drained dry. I need stuff for me, too. I am going to compare apples and oranges. I will watch what people do and look at stereotypes. I don't ignore what I see, and I am not ashamed of it. If people judge me, I am quick to correct if you got me wrong. However, if you state it right and it is the way I am, then I stand correct - you are right.

Judgment doesn't stop anything for me, and it should not stop you, either. I am not listening to everyone's judgments, but I do listen to those who make sense and can contribute to my life. What do you think? Do you see what I am saying about judgment and the necessity to judge?

When people say something about me that is true, and I don't like it, it makes me hungrier. I don't pay attention to people just complaining and nagging. I look for the truth and change what I don't like about me. If I am rejected for something, I want to know why. I want to be the best I can be because I want things in life.

So if you hear things you don't like, don't get sad or stay sad for long. Use it as fuel to make you better and improve your life. If you are rejected, come back with a vengeance and make it happen. Come get it, come hell or high water. Don't let up unless you say it makes sense to let it go. That's cool, too.

Let Go of Judgment

If you don't overcome other people's judgments of you, or if you are in denial about what is true about you, you are going to look like Boo Boo the Fool. The lady who was stuck earlier in this chapter was in denial that she was the reason her situation wouldn't change. If she wants to be broke with a bachelor's degree, an education, and living in America, what can I say?

If I think that it is me and not someone else with a problem, I am judging if they are Oprah, Jeff, Mark, or Steve type of people. If you don't have it going like that, I don't know how much there is you can teach me. If you don't have a pot to piss in or a window to throw it out of, I don't give a doggone. If you say my book doesn't work, but you paid the $25 for it, I am not given a refund because I am proof it does work! And I said what I said!!

For the people who have settled on failing in life, they have let it go. They let go of their dreams, and I am not going to baby them out of it. They need to grow up out of it. It is time for them to let go of stinking thinking instead of thinking people are going to feel sorry for them and give it to them. I am not.

I will tell you now: I am not going to beat down your door to convince you what is possible for you. I let people go, so if you are not ready, I will leave and get on. I know someone is out there who wants what I have and is ready to take that step and that's where I will be.

I want to be around winners, not people with a ton of excuses for why they can't. I am not settling for failure sitting around going broke. I am a winner, and I

Melvina W.

am making my winner's circle.

If you think you can walk off a bridge and survive, you go on right ahead. I am going to stay here ten toes down, and there are only a few people I would jump in front of and say, "Look, are we sure you are going to do this?" Because at the end of the day, you are grown, you can do what you like and have to make your own decisions. I understand the assignment, and even with my children, sometimes I have to watch the consequences of their and other people's decisions.

I let it go because I know the proof is in the pudding. Did you put sugar and needed items in there? I don't know why people think we should feel bad about something happening to others. I know how it feels to experience loss, poverty, and struggle.

I cannot say that I am moved to give away my money because people are going through bad times. You will get more by having a plan from me than coming here with a sob story. Too many people got them, and they don't lead to progress but a life lived full of excuses. I like people who are moving, and you don't know what they are going through or have been through based on their work ethic.

Their journey is more powerful when you see them make it in spite of the problems rather than pointing to them for sympathy. I was more moved by the person with progress than tears. I am just saying the one who will have more to show in a few years is often the one with a plan and not tears.

Let Go of Judgment
 Moving on.

When You are Not Appreciated

I have to tell you, if people are trying to rattle your cage, you have to let it go! This chapter is for women, especially because as women, wives, mothers, and friends, we can feel unappreciated. Oftentimes, the feeling is warranted and makes sense when you are not getting acknowledged for what you do.

We work hard, and that work is not always appreciated because people feel like you should do what you are doing. Children often will tell their mother, "You are supposed to do that for me. You are my mother." They do not consider that abortion is a law for women who don't want to do anything for children.

Some laws permit babies that are born to be aborted if the woman does not want the child as late as 8 months or even if the child is born! Now, I wouldn't go this far, but this is an option that women can choose. Children need to be reminded that being here is a choice they made.

Melvina W.

There is no rule that forces us to have to bear children, stay home, cook, and clean for little people all day. Social norms have been changing over several decades to level out the responsibilities of men and women to both have to provide financially and work outside the house. So why is it that both parents have the responsibility, but only one of them is expected to cook, clean, stay home, and raise children?

This is one of the old-school myths I did not agree with in Christianity. These old rules will say that women are supposed to do this or that and not have what they want in life. I used to fight with what I believed, and then I stopped. I stopped fighting who I am and embraced my truth, and that I am not a Christian.

I am a woman of faith, yes, but I do not identify with the ideologies many Christians have about life. I don't believe my lot in life is to stay home and take care of children and lose sight of my goals and purpose. I am important, too, and why should my dreams be cast aside for his dreams? What makes him more important than me if we are both equal partners in this marriage.

We are both bringing in money. We are both spending time. We both have to lay down to make the baby, but I have to carry the baby for nine months. If anything, I should be able to take a longer vacation after the baby is born if we are talking about fairness. This is what I thought logically, but I know life doesn't work like that, does it?

Women are expected to breastfeed for as long as possible for the benefit of the baby. This means

When You Are Not Appreciated

that I am sacrificing the look and feel of my breasts to feed a child that one day will grow up and tell me how they don't need me. How many women out there have children who told them this or heard, "I don't need you, Momma. I can make my own decisions." This is a slap in the face to a mother because we gave our body, time, and resources to raise children, and when they are not grateful or appreciative, it does rub you all the wrong ways.

It is not unreasonable for a woman to grow angry with the people who have missed her sacrifice and downplay her frustration with the lack of respect. There are the mothers who will not be held accountable for their decisions to govern their children, but what about the mothers who did things right and the children give them their behind to kiss? Who or what speaks up for them?

I raise my hand and say I will speak for the women, the wives, and those who have given to children and families–or anyone else and were not appreciated. I know how much work it takes to raise one child, and I have three children, two of which are a pair of twins. So I get it. We had double duty with our girls because they each had other special needs we had to attend to, and creating an individual plan for each of them took work and effort.

I made sure to go to bat for my girls and give them what they needed in school to have equal opportunities. I was born half-deaf, and unfortunately, I passed the hearing loss down to my twin girls. It is not easy raising a child who is set up to need to pivot and be open to other ways of handling life. We won't always know what they need, but we will be guilty of doing our best. Sometimes, we make mistakes and we can feel like we need to live out our days apologizing to them.

I see parents chasing behind their children, trying to get the confirmation or approval of their parenting. Stop that right now. Chasing your tail like a dog is not going to get you a different result. If your children are in their feelings and they are grown, let it go. Yes, you can be there for them and remind them you love them, but if they take a step away from you, allow them to live out their decision.

It can be hard to see those we love turn their backs on us, but that is the role of a parent. As a mother, I can say that nothing can hurt like this kind of rejection or oversight can hit a woman's heart. We are humans, and we love our children like any other mother in the animal kingdom. We will give our lives for them; many of us have given up our lives to see them happy.

We have stopped attending school and used our last bit of money on something they needed or wanted, and it makes us feel good to do it. However, the pain many of us are carrying in life is of our choosing. I know you might say, "No, it's not. Why would I choose this?" But we can as mothers. We can choose to hold on to burdens that are not ours and deal with stuff that we need to let the hell go!

Too often as mothers, we will go through cycles of abuse and keep chasing our tails to save our children. Our children give us their behind to kiss, but we are still

When You Are Not Appreciated

giving them our best. These children will forget about your birthday, skip holidays, and they can live down your hallway and don't want to lift a finger to help you!

There is a popular saying that I think of as I type this, "Don't cry for me when I am gone. I am living right now, and you won't even say hello." Nevertheless, they spend time with us, but they spend more time with their friends whom they could have just met like they love them more than their parents.

They will work a job and quit a job so that you can work and take care of them. You tell them what they need to do, and they get mad at you and start slamming your doors. They tell you to treat them like an adult, but they are not taking on any of the real responsibility. These children feel that life is unfair because they are not making enough money to care for themselves.

They don't look for solutions, though. They instead lean on their parents and expect them to offset their financial problems. It is unappreciative to live off your parents and not speak to them when you live in their house. It is equally wrong to see your parents struggling, and you are unbothered by it. How can you fix your mouth to eat your momma's food and not think to wash the dishes or ask if she needs something?

We have children out here acting like they are your man! This is why some women will not get married or can't keep a happy home. It's because you are allowing your children to tear it up. You are not making people appreciate you so they not only disrespect you,

Melvina W.

but anything attached to you.

Can you blame the man if he is tired of your children when you didn't give them a proper balance in your life? What is that man supposed to do or say to your children that you won't fight him over or it won't cause some problems? He doesn't have to be the step daddy either; he can try to be, and there is a disconnect if no one can tell your children anything, not even you.

If your children start complaining about how their job is stressful because it doesn't pay enough, that is not your problem. Their suffering can lead to depression, and they can repeat this for 10 and 20 years if you don't check this at the door. You need to stop being nice and be a parent. You must teach them responsibility, respect, and how to listen to authority and take direction. They will not make it out here if you keep doing everything for them.

Remember, you are not their friend or homegirl. You are their mother or father, THEIR PARENTS! STOP ACTING like you and your grown children are equal. YOU ARE NOT!!

How does a parent aid in their own suffering? By cooking for them when they are grown. You put in twenty-some-odd years already, why are you cooking more than here and there when they are grown? Don't say they have children! You are the grandma, not the mother; they are quick to point out that they're the mother; let them do it.

What would they be doing if you weren't there?

When You Are Not Appreciated

Figuring it out. So why not allow them to do it while you are in good health, still can find your dreams, and do what you want in life? Stop allowing their stress to be yours! You can't do laundry for them anymore. You are not their wife, father, or their man. I don't know too many fathers doing that anyway. But you are not their spouse. You are a parent to an adult child now.

Your baby is growing up, and you have to let them fly the nest. These same children won't do the same for you, so how can you make this make sense in your head or your heart? You have to see that they don't appreciate you, and I know it is not easy. I have cried about stuff like this too, because we all go through it.

To make things worse, if you are doing all you need to for the children and yourself, but he can't remember the anniversary, you might feel like you want to choke somebody. When we are hurt and feel overlooked, it can turn a house upside down. You can blow up on little things because the big thing is that you don't feel appreciated. You feel like a doormat everyone wipes their feet on, and no one offers to clean.

You are muddy, beat down, and in desperate need of attention, but your voice is too low. The only time they act like they miss you or see you is when you don't do something. So you have a negative reinforcement situation going on that associates your presence with a to-do list. When we feel like this, we can withdraw personally and shut ourselves off from the ones we live with.

We can be present, but our hearts are far away.

Melvina W.

We can cook, clean, and do the work of a mother and wife, but we are absent from the body. It's like we are a walking zombie and a shadow of who we used to be. Please don't believe that this is your lot in life. That there is nothing more for you to obtain and have.

You are not a maid. You are a woman who wants to be appreciated. You want to feel like a woman and be made to love like a woman. These are things that are reasonable, and you deserve.

I can tell you, I don't speak with my daughters every day or as often as I like. I remember all of their birthdays and holidays. I used to go all out, but I am realizing maybe that is too much, and I should respond with the same level of interest they have in celebrating these holidays with me. I am done doing all the big stuff like shopping sprees to blow a couple thousand dollars on each of them. Or giving them money to pay a bill as a gift. Now, I send them a gift card of $25 or $50 because I am lucky to get anything in return. I am clearly meeting them where they are with me.

I remember I sent them flowers for Valentine's Day. To each of their homes or on their job, I sent them flowers from Glenn and me. Because no matter how old they get, we, their parents will always be their first love. When we saw them, we knew we would love them all their lives, and we still do. It was hurtful that when my birthday came around, not one of my daughters sent me a card, an e-card, a text, or made a call to tell me "Happy Birthday."

I don't feel appreciated when things like this

When You Are Not Appreciated

happen, but I learned to LET IT GO! Yes, I know they love us, but I don't understand how everything you do and still do for your children, they can dismiss on the count of a few bad moments from the past. Everything I built, I built, and plan to leave for my daughters–things are always subject to change. Because I always keep the ball in my court. Things can always change, so we will see.

With the grown children, you might only get one that calls her parents to wish a Happy Birthday, even though we gave them life! It is a hard pill to swallow when you are left in the shadows or are not a priority to the ones you prioritize. So I get it, and it was hard as hell to let them go so they could grow up in this sense. Sometimes families grow up together, and sometimes they drift apart. It wouldn't be on my account, but maybe we became too different or we are too much the same?

But, you will find on the job you can deal with people who don't appreciate you all the same. As a medical coder, trainer, and mentor, you don't know how much lip I have to deal with when people talk back about stuff they say I don't know. I used to be a 40k-a-year medical coder. I used to be a 50k and 70k earner a year. It took time to get to six figures and make what I do today, and I met many who didn't appreciate my journey.

You have people who want to say all of your accomplishments are based on your age or your personality, but it was based on my work. I worked hard for this and not everyone will choose to see that. It is not that the proof is not in the pudding. It is there. People can see it and read about it, but what they choose to see is a whole nother matter.

You can't make people see the truth or accept it and many will see it and not care. They don't value what you do and can overlook your accomplishments. At work they can know about your degrees and still try to treat you like a newcomer. To say the least, it is disrespectful to be absent-minded about what I can bring to the table.

I am sure as hell not going to bend over and kiss some raw butts. I worked hard and I won't take too well with people being unappreciative of me. Like I told you, I am the most important person to me, even if others don't see it. The way you allow people to treat you is a reflection of how you see yourself. You don't want people to see you as a fool. Now you know why I let people go. I can't deal with it because I know I will still be here and survive.

On the job, I have had to let people go and I was let go. If I worked 5 years somewhere and they fired me, I feel like I would still survive. I have been living for over 45 years without you, so I will be alright. I know a person who I helped get a job and coached for many years. Things were fine when she thought I would accept anything from her.

When I had to turn up the heat because she was slipping, she got mad at me and tried to talk crazy to me. You know that all I did to help her get a job, keep her job, and learn what she needed to excel, she took

When You Are Not Appreciated

a crap on. She left out of my life, and when she lef,t it was mutual that we had nothing else to talk about. Funny thing, she is still friends with my daughters, but she and I haven't exchanged words in years and it will stay that way for all the years to come. See, I LET HER GO!

It's not just what you do for your family that can go unappreciated, but also what you do for those you work with or for. When I feel the most unappreciated is when people who have done nothing for me and I did everything for them are ungrateful. When I hear people tell me, "You haven't done nothing for me," and I know that I have, my response is nothing.

I walk away from these people. I think, "Who the hell are you that I should do something for you, now?" If you didn't appreciate everything I already did, you best believe I am not lifting another finger to help you. I won't make your life difficult. I will just remove myself. I tell those people to lose my number, if they had my address, lose that and my email. I am good if we never speak again, and I mean it. I stand on business with that!

I fired a contractor who used to do my landscaping because he started to become unappreciative. I used to pay this many thousands of dollars, like over 8k to cut down trees and do other odd and end things I needed for my property. He was okay at these assignments but I could have hired anybody. I look out for people who I appreciate, and they appreciate me.

I want to believe that the feeling is mutual, but when I realize it is not, I let it go. I fired this contractor

Melvina W.

because I told them, after writing them nearly 10k for a job, if he asked me for another dollar, it would be the last dollar he got from me. He thought I was joking or stupid. I know how much the job cost, and I was okay with paying a little more because we were working together.

A contractor for over five years lost tens of thousands of dollars over less than $400. Can you believe that? I am not saying I wouldn't pay it. I just didn't want to pay it that day. Clearly, I got the money, but I don't like when anyone tries to bully me. When he got that $400 dollars and that job finished, I deleted his number and blocked him! He was LET GO!

There was nothing else to say. He tried to call me and say he would do things for the yard for free, but I told him, "I got someone else, and that would not be necessary. Your services are no longer needed. Please lose my number."

When people try to get mad at me for something they say I didn't do, I ask the questions they wished I wouldn't have. "So, what have you done with your life that you need my help now? What happened to your plan? Did you go to school to increase your salary? What have you put together that can show me what I need to do for you?" My own daughters don't even call me asking for help or money. So everyone else better take a page from them...I mean that!

When people say I don't do anything for them, I am going to make sure it stays that way. I would tell them to keep doing what they are doing, and I am going

When You Are Not Appreciated

to do what I do. We will see how that works out for you. I know how it will work out for me, I will be just fine.

People who are ungrateful, spoiled, entitled, and cannot see past the negative to see the good, there is nothing I can do. If you don't see any good out of what I am putting down then we have nothing else to talk about. I am a reasonable person, I speak common sense and I enjoy the conversation. It makes sense in every facet of life to be appreciative of others.

Gratitude is passing it forward. When you are grateful it does something to your heart and makes you want to give to others. I enjoy passing it forward and sharing what I have with people who are appreciative. You can get more when you are grateful than complaining about every doggone thing. Nothing in life is perfect, so you have to know when to let it go.

I am quick to take inventory of the people who appreciate me. On the job, I look at my bank account. I want to see how many zeros are being added, and I know how much they care. The more zeros I would say the more because I appreciate this language. I speak this language because I need money to do what I want and need to do. In relationships, it would be time and the things people do for me that I don't ask for. If I ask and they do it, that is fine, but I am grateful for what people do that I don't ask for because that was out of their own heart. It can mean more sometimes.

It is wonderful to feel appreciated, and it is a mutual benefit. People want to do more for you as you

Melvina W.

keep showing your gratitude. But what you should look out for is when that gratitude changes to obligation. When people stop saying thank you, please, and all the manners go away. When people start feeding you BS and think you will eat it because you like or love them.

Very rarely will I be abused because when I see it miles away, I am already thinking about getting away. While you think you are reeling me in like toilet paper, I will be reeling you the "F"f out of my life. Shoot, I will soak the whole roll in water and toss you out with the cardboard and not wait for the ending. That part!!

When I am in pain, I am bold about it. I am bold because I am dealing with it. I am not in denial. If someone offends me, I am going to say and be loud about it. If you don't know, you will know about it first. I gave the contractor a chance, and he burned the bridge. Being a scary cat in the corner is not going to get anything done.

A lot of conversations like this can be uncomfortable, I know. With me, when I am bold and direct, some people squirm and try to get away from the truth, but I am not running. If you want to have a conversation we can until I am done. A lot of these conversations don't go as expected because to me, a conversation doesn't mean things have to be over.

You might not know you offended me. You might not know how I feel. You might be guessing what you did that caused the problem. I am grown enough to tell you with the intention for us to work it out like adults.

When You Are Not Appreciated

If you get your panties in a bunch and you can't talk anymore, get an attitude and storm off and stuff like that. I will not be kissing your behind or signing up to be your loony tune. I am not desperate for work or friends; I am going to be alright.

You have to be you. If being you is too much for people, put them out of their misery and stop talking to them. I don't force myself on anybody. I am who I am. I talk loud because I have been partially deaf all my life. If I talk low, I cannot hear you or myself. So you gotta give me something to work with.

Growing up how I did, I had to speak up for myself. I had to be loud so I was heard because I know what it is like to not be seen. Growing up in the South as a dark skin black girl was not easy or common, and it didn't give me sympathy. I cried many nights for the names people called me and how others treated me. That didn't make me weaker, though, because I didn't let it. It makes me stronger. So, if people treat me well or badly, I know how to make it work for Melvina.

I learned how to let people go and how to get the hell on. When you stick around too long, you will know. They will start yelling at you and getting in their feelings. They will exchange words that are delivered with their neck rolling and lips popping. They crack me up when they start clapping their hands when they talk and rolling their eyes. If they start cutting me off and getting rude, I start being quiet.

I don't get angry. I don't change my personality because that is beneath me. I have choices and options, and I don't have to be where they are. I can move. I normally say, "Okay, well, let me leave."

If they are at my house, it is even simpler. I go to my front door and open it. They already know what I mean. Get out. Keep reading with me; LET IT GO!

I let go of negativity, I let go of voting democratic, and I am not going to church with you. If someone has told you that you cannot let people or family go. I am here to be a living witness that, "Yes, you can."

I let a lot of people go and there isn't a person or situation that I couldn't. We have choices, and if you rob yourself of the choice, know that is still your choice. Nobody is forcing you to put up with their mess. You are choosing to put up with it.

Anyone who is toxic and got drama, or on drugs, in and out of jail, they are the bad apple in the bunch. They are going to be in another bunch, not mine. Now, for my children, they are the exception. But make no mistake, I will let go of their attitudes, and if they only want to talk to me once a year or no more, I can deal with that too. I cannot let them go and stop caring, but I can and will let go of any toxic behaviors with them, for real

I raised them to have what they need. They have what they need: their own houses, cars, and phones. If all I gotta do is deal with attitudes and differences of opinions, I am good with that. Over in my heart, I am being positive and sharing love with diplomacy. I will never be their friend, I will not kiss their butts, and I

When You Are Not Appreciated
will always be their mother.

My marriage also has expectations. If that were to fall apart at any time and we don't have this positive and healthy relationship because it is toxic, I can let that go too. I don't foresee that of course, but there is no one above being let go in Melvina's world! Sometimes, it is the situation you let go of. Sometimes, it is the person. Sometimes, it is how you see it, and you choose to LET IT GO.

How you spend your time is also how you choose what you let go. If you spend time with people this is how you are choosing what you want in life. Where you spend your time is what you value. If you are spending your time with people or on things you don't want to be as important in your life, you need to make some changes.

If you don't know what you want, go back to the previous chapter and make the list to figure it out. You are going to have more problems if you don't know who you are. I cannot repeat this enough because it is so easy to skip. We can think through the questions and come up with the politically correct answers and live miserably. I know I am a challenge, and I don't care.

I have standards and things I want and need. I have no problem with demanding them. I have things I expect, and I want them to be respected. If a person chooses not to regard my expectations, I can move on and let it go. If you have not gotten to that point where you can or know when you should let things go, you need to read these last two chapters closely. We are

Melvina W.

almost done with this thang.

You cannot be honest with no one if you cannot be honest with things within yourself. You will miss every red flag. A red flag, I would say, is too many mistakes. If you are fifty years old and can't rub two nickels together, you have a problem. That is a big red flag. If you're gonna blame it on others, let me stop you. It's likely your children are grown, so what the hell happened?

What are you doing? Saving everyone else but letting yourself sink? While you are taking care of others, who is going to take care of you? Who is bothered by what you need? And you still feel like you need to run around with a cape on your back when you don't have anything for yourself?

How many times are you going to let someone cuss you out and treat you terribly? I mean, got dang. How long are you going to give the excuse you are their mother? Are you their correctional officer, pastor, wife, and everything else too? Let them grow up and go live how they want to and suffer the consequences. Nothing teaches us lessons faster than consequences.

You can give people chances. I believe in that. I don't give too many chances in business, if I am honest. Second chances are not common because I realized by experience those who got the second chance still ended up fired. So, I usually skip the semantics and get it over with rather than drag it out.

As for my family, my husband and daughters get

When You Are Not Appreciated

about fifty million chances. It depends on what we are talking about, but it does come with consequences. It is an intervention where you have to earn the chance and work towards it. This is not a freebie; you have to come and fight for it for me.

Make them work to keep you around. If they are not willing to work to get back to appreciate your presence, cut them off and leave them there. If you are doing it big in your business and making over a 100k a year, I doubt your best friend will be someone on Section Eight living off food stamps. If you have a doctorate, I am also sure your bestie is not someone who can't formulate a complete thought, read, or write. What are you going to have to do to nurse this relationship? Do everything for them?

We don't have time for that in life, that takes too much time, and too many are not appreciative of your time. They think people owe them something because they built their lives on others, giving them what they need to survive. I believe in being accountable, getting out here, and making it happen. Staying at home, playing games, and living off food stamps and welfare is not something I feel is the American Dream. We are in the land of opportunity, and that means going to work.

We have to work for anything we want in life, from relationships to money. There are going to be the people who won't get up to the plate to bat. Some got up to the plate and didn't perform. You gotta let them go, and you shouldn't worry about it. If they can't perform or don't appreciate you, why waste your energy to talk?

Melvina W.

I have people I won't even speak to if they say hello to me. You wouldn't know we ever knew each other because I don't want to waste any more time or energy on people who mean no good to me. Appreciation and gratitude go hand in hand. We're moving on…

When You Are Not Appreciated

Stop Overanalyzing

I have to tell you, if people are trying to rattle your cage, you have to let it go! This chapter is for women, especially because as women, wives, mothers, and friends, we can feel unappreciated. Oftentimes, the feeling is warranted and makes sense when you are not getting acknowledged for what you do.

We work hard, and that work is not always appreciated because people feel like you should do what you are doing. Children often will tell their mother, "You are supposed to do that for me. You are my mother." They do not consider that abortion is a law for women who don't want to do anything for children.

Some laws permit babies that are born to be aborted if the woman does not want the child as late as 8 months or even if the child is born! Now, I wouldn't go this far, but this is an option that women can choose. Children need to be reminded that being here is a choice they made.

Melvina W.

There is no rule that forces us to have to bear children, stay home, cook, and clean for little people all day. Social norms have been changing over several decades to level out the responsibilities of men and women to both have to provide financially and work outside the house. So why is it that both parents have the responsibility, but only one of them is expected to cook, clean, stay home, and raise children?

This is one of the old-school myths I did not agree with in Christianity. These old rules will say that women are supposed to do this or that and not have what they want in life. I used to fight with what I believed, and then I stopped. I stopped fighting who I am and embraced my truth, and that I am not a Christian.

I am a woman of faith, yes, but I do not identify with the ideologies many Christians have about life. I don't believe my lot in life is to stay home and take care of children and lose sight of my goals and purpose. I am important, too, and why should my dreams be cast aside for his dreams? What makes him more important than me if we are both equal partners in this marriage.

We are both bringing in money. We are both spending time. We both have to lay down to make the baby, but I have to carry the baby for nine months. If anything, I should be able to take a longer vacation after the baby is born if we are talking about fairness. This is what I thought logically, but I know life doesn't work like that, does it?

Women are expected to breastfeed for as long as possible for the benefit of the baby. This means that I am sacrificing the look and feel of my breasts to feed a child that one day will grow up and tell me how they don't need me. How many women out there have children who told them this or heard, "I don't need you, Momma. I can make my own decisions." This is a slap in the face to a mother because we gave our body, time, and resources to raise children, and when they are not grateful or appreciative, it does rub you all the wrong ways.

It is not unreasonable for a woman to grow angry with the people who have missed her sacrifice and downplay her frustration with the lack of respect. There are the mothers who will not be held accountable for their decisions to govern their children, but what about the mothers who did things right and the children give them their behind to kiss? Who or what speaks up for them?

I raise my hand and say I will speak for the women, the wives, and those who have given to children and families–or anyone else and were not appreciated. I know how much work it takes to raise one child, and I have three children, two of which are a pair of twins. So I get it. We had double duty with our girls because they each had other special needs we had to attend to, and creating an individual plan for each of them took work and effort.

I made sure to go to bat for my girls and give them what they needed in school to have equal opportunities. I was born half-deaf, and unfortunately, I passed the hearing loss down to my twin girls. It is not easy raising a child who is set up to need to pivot and be open to other ways of handling life. We won't always know what they need, but we will be guilty of doing our best. Sometimes, we make mistakes and we can feel like we need to live out our days apologizing to them.

I see parents chasing behind their children, trying to get the confirmation or approval of their parenting. Stop that right now. Chasing your tail like a dog is not going to get you a different result. If your children are in their feelings and they are grown, let it go. Yes, you can be there for them and remind them you love them, but if they take a step away from you, allow them to live out their decision.

It can be hard to see those we love turn their backs on us, but that is the role of a parent. As a mother, I can say that nothing can hurt like this kind of rejection or oversight can hit a woman's heart. We are humans, and we love our children like any other mother in the animal kingdom. We will give our lives for them; many of us have given up our lives to see them happy.

We have stopped attending school and used our last bit of money on something they needed or wanted, and it makes us feel good to do it. However, the pain many of us are carrying in life is of our choosing. I know you might say, "No, it's not. Why would I choose this?" But we can as mothers. We can choose to hold on to burdens that are not ours and deal with stuff that we need to let the hell go!

Too often as mothers, we will go through cycles of abuse and keep chasing our tails to save our children. Our children give us their behind to kiss, but we are still giving them our best. These children will forget about your birthday, skip holidays, and they can live down your hallway and don't want to lift a finger to help you!

There is a popular saying that I think of as I type this, "Don't cry for me when I am gone. I am living right now, and you won't even say hello." Nevertheless, they spend time with us, but they spend more time with their friends whom they could have just met like they love them more than their parents.

They will work a job and quit a job so that you can work and take care of them. You tell them what they need to do, and they get mad at you and start slamming your doors. They tell you to treat them like an adult, but they are not taking on any of the real responsibility. These children feel that life is unfair because they are not making enough money to care for themselves.

They don't look for solutions, though. They instead lean on their parents and expect them to offset their financial problems. It is unappreciative to live off your parents and not speak to them when you live in their house. It is equally wrong to see your parents struggling, and you are unbothered by it. How can you fix your mouth to eat your momma's food and not think to wash the dishes or ask if she needs something?

We have children out here acting like they are your man! This is why some women will not get married or can't keep a happy home. It's because you are allowing your children to tear it up. You are not making people appreciate you so they not only disrespect you, but anything attached to you.

Can you blame the man if he is tired of your children when you didn't give them a proper balance in your life? What is that man supposed to do or say to your children that you won't fight him over or it won't cause some problems? He doesn't have to be the step daddy either; he can try to be, and there is a disconnect if no one can tell your children anything, not even you.

If your children start complaining about how their job is stressful because it doesn't pay enough, that is not your problem. Their suffering can lead to depression, and they can repeat this for 10 and 20 years if you don't check this at the door. You need to stop being nice and be a parent. You must teach them responsibility, respect, and how to listen to authority and take direction. They will not make it out here if you keep doing everything for them.

Remember, you are not their friend or homegirl. You are their mother or father, THEIR PARENTS! STOP ACTING like you and your grown children are equal. YOU ARE NOT!!

How does a parent aid in their own suffering? By cooking for them when they are grown. You put in twenty-some-odd years already, why are you cooking more than here and there when they are grown? Don't say they have children! You are the grandma, not the mother; they are quick to point out that they're the mother; let them do it.

What would they be doing if you weren't there?

Stop Overanalyzing

Figuring it out. So why not allow them to do it while you are in good health, still can find your dreams, and do what you want in life? Stop allowing their stress to be yours! You can't do laundry for them anymore. You are not their wife, father, or their man. I don't know too many fathers doing that anyway. But you are not their spouse. You are a parent to an adult child now.

Your baby is growing up, and you have to let them fly the nest. These same children won't do the same for you, so how can you make this make sense in your head or your heart? You have to see that they don't appreciate you, and I know it is not easy. I have cried about stuff like this too, because we all go through it.

To make things worse, if you are doing all you need to for the children and yourself, but he can't remember the anniversary, you might feel like you want to choke somebody. When we are hurt and feel overlooked, it can turn a house upside down. You can blow up on little things because the big thing is that you don't feel appreciated. You feel like a doormat everyone wipes their feet on, and no one offers to clean.

You are muddy, beat down, and in desperate need of attention, but your voice is too low. The only time they act like they miss you or see you is when you don't do something. So you have a negative reinforcement situation going on that associates your presence with a to-do list. When we feel like this, we can withdraw personally and shut ourselves off from the ones we live with.

We can be present, but our hearts are far away.

Melvina W.

We can cook, clean, and do the work of a mother and wife, but we are absent from the body. It's like we are a walking zombie and a shadow of who we used to be. Please don't believe that this is your lot in life. That there is nothing more for you to obtain and have.

You are not a maid. You are a woman who wants to be appreciated. You want to feel like a woman and be made to love like a woman. These are things that are reasonable, and you deserve.

I can tell you, I don't speak with my daughters every day or as often as I like. I remember all of their birthdays and holidays. I used to go all out, but I am realizing maybe that is too much, and I should respond with the same level of interest they have in celebrating these holidays with me. I am done doing all the big stuff like shopping sprees to blow a couple thousand dollars on each of them. Or giving them money to pay a bill as a gift. Now, I send them a gift card of $25 or $50 because I am lucky to get anything in return. I am clearly meeting them where they are with me.

I remember I sent them flowers for Valentine's Day. To each of their homes or on their job, I sent them flowers from Glenn and me. Because no matter how old they get, we, their parents will always be their first love. When we saw them, we knew we would love them all their lives, and we still do. It was hurtful that when my birthday came around, not one of my daughters sent me a card, an e-card, a text, or made a call to tell me "Happy Birthday."

I don't feel appreciated when things like this

happen, but I learned to LET IT GO! Yes, I know they love us, but I don't understand how everything you do and still do for your children, they can dismiss on the count of a few bad moments from the past. Everything I built, I built, and plan to leave for my daughters–things are always subject to change. Because I always keep the ball in my court. Things can always change, so we will see.

With the grown children, you might only get one that calls her parents to wish a Happy Birthday, even though we gave them life! It is a hard pill to swallow when you are left in the shadows or are not a priority to the ones you prioritize. So I get it, and it was hard as hell to let them go so they could grow up in this sense. Sometimes families grow up together, and sometimes they drift apart. It wouldn't be on my account, but maybe we became too different or we are too much the same?

But, you will find on the job you can deal with people who don't appreciate you all the same. As a medical coder, trainer, and mentor, you don't know how much lip I have to deal with when people talk back about stuff they say I don't know. I used to be a 40k-a-year medical coder. I used to be a 50k and 70k earner a year. It took time to get to six figures and make what I do today, and I met many who didn't appreciate my journey.

You have people who want to say all of your accomplishments are based on your age or your personality, but it was based on my work. I worked hard for this and not everyone will choose to see that. It is not that the proof is not in the pudding. It is there. People can see it and read about it, but what they choose to see is a whole nother matter.

You can't make people see the truth or accept it and many will see it and not care. They don't value what you do and can overlook your accomplishments. At work they can know about your degrees and still try to treat you like a newcomer. To say the least, it is disrespectful to be absent-minded about what I can bring to the table.

I am sure as hell not going to bend over and kiss some raw butts. I worked hard and I won't take too well with people being unappreciative of me. Like I told you, I am the most important person to me, even if others don't see it. The way you allow people to treat you is a reflection of how you see yourself. You don't want people to see you as a fool. Now you know why I let people go. I can't deal with it because I know I will still be here and survive.

On the job, I have had to let people go and I was let go. If I worked 5 years somewhere and they fired me, I feel like I would still survive. I have been living for over 45 years without you, so I will be alright. I know a person who I helped get a job and coached for many years. Things were fine when she thought I would accept anything from her.

When I had to turn up the heat because she was slipping, she got mad at me and tried to talk crazy to me. You know that all I did to help her get a job, keep her job, and learn what she needed to excel, she took a crap on. She left out of my life, and when she left it was mutual that we had nothing else to talk about. Funny thing, she is still friends with my daughters, but she and I haven't exchanged words in years and it will stay that way for all the years to come. See, I LET HER GO!

It's not just what you do for your family that can go unappreciated, but also what you do for those you work with or for. When I feel the most unappreciated is when people who have done nothing for me and I did everything for them are ungrateful. When I hear people tell me, "You haven't done nothing for me," and I know that I have, my response is nothing.

I walk away from these people. I think, "Who the hell are you that I should do something for you, now?" If you didn't appreciate everything I already did, you best believe I am not lifting another finger to help you. I won't make your life difficult. I will just remove myself. I tell those people to lose my number, if they had my address, lose that and my email. I am good if we never speak again, and I mean it. I stand on business with that!

I fired a contractor who used to do my landscaping because he started to become unappreciative. I used to pay this many thousands of dollars, like over 8k to cut down trees and do other odd and end things I needed for my property. He was okay at these assignments but I could have hired anybody. I look out for people who I appreciate, and they appreciate me.

I want to believe that the feeling is mutual, but when I realize it is not, I let it go. I fired this contractor

Melvina W.

because I told them, after writing them nearly 10k for a job, if he asked me for another dollar, it would be the last dollar he got from me. He thought I was joking or stupid. I know how much the job cost, and I was okay with paying a little more because we were working together.

A contractor for over five years lost tens of thousands of dollars over less than $400. Can you believe that? I am not saying I wouldn't pay it. I just didn't want to pay it that day. Clearly, I got the money, but I don't like when anyone tries to bully me. When he got that $400 dollars and that job finished, I deleted his number and blocked him! He was LET GO!

There was nothing else to say. He tried to call me and say he would do things for the yard for free, but I told him, "I got someone else, and that would not be necessary. Your services are no longer needed. Please lose my number."

When people try to get mad at me for something they say I didn't do, I ask the questions they wished I wouldn't have. "So, what have you done with your life that you need my help now? What happened to your plan? Did you go to school to increase your salary? What have you put together that can show me what I need to do for you?" My own daughters don't even call me asking for help or money. So everyone else better take a page from them...I mean that!

When people say I don't do anything for them, I am going to make sure it stays that way. I would tell them to keep doing what they are doing, and I am going to do what I do. We will see how that works out for you. I know how it will work out for me, I will be just fine.

People who are ungrateful, spoiled, entitled, and cannot see past the negative to see the good, there is nothing I can do. If you don't see any good out of what I am putting down then we have nothing else to talk about. I am a reasonable person, I speak common sense and I enjoy the conversation. It makes sense in every facet of life to be appreciative of others.

Gratitude is passing it forward. When you are grateful it does something to your heart and makes you want to give to others. I enjoy passing it forward and sharing what I have with people who are appreciative. You can get more when you are grateful than complaining about every doggone thing. Nothing in life is perfect, so you have to know when to let it go.

I am quick to take inventory of the people who appreciate me. On the job, I look at my bank account. I want to see how many zeros are being added, and I know how much they care. The more zeros I would say the more because I appreciate this language. I speak this language because I need money to do what I want and need to do. In relationships, it would be time and the things people do for me that I don't ask for. If I ask and they do it, that is fine, but I am grateful for what people do that I don't ask for because that was out of their own heart. It can mean more sometimes.

It is wonderful to feel appreciated, and it is a mutual benefit. People want to do more for you as you keep showing your gratitude. But what you should look out for is when that gratitude changes to obligation. When people stop saying thank you, please, and all the manners go away. When people start feeding you BS and think you will eat it because you like or love them.

Very rarely will I be abused because when I see it miles away, I am already thinking about getting away. While you think you are reeling me in like toilet paper, I will be reeling you the "F" out of my life. Shoot, I will soak the whole roll in water and toss you out with the cardboard and not wait for the ending. That part!!

When I am in pain, I am bold about it. I am bold because I am dealing with it. I am not in denial. If someone offends me, I am going to say and be loud about it. If you don't know, you will know about it first. I gave the contractor a chance, and he burned the bridge. Being a scary cat in the corner is not going to get anything done.

A lot of conversations like this can be uncomfortable, I know. With me, when I am bold and direct, some people squirm and try to get away from the truth, but I am not running. If you want to have a conversation we can until I am done. A lot of these conversations don't go as expected because to me, a conversation doesn't mean things have to be over.

You might not know you offended me. You might not know how I feel. You might be guessing what you did that caused the problem. I am grown enough to tell you with the intention for us to work it out like adults.

Stop Overanalyzing

If you get your panties in a bunch and you can't talk anymore, get an attitude and storm off and stuff like that. I will not be kissing your behind or signing up to be your loony tune. I am not desperate for work or friends; I am going to be alright.

You have to be you. If being you is too much for people, put them out of their misery and stop talking to them. I don't force myself on anybody. I am who I am. I talk loud because I have been partially deaf all my life. If I talk low, I cannot hear you or myself. So you gotta give me something to work with.

myself. I had to be loud so I was heard because I know what it is like to not be seen. Growing up in the South as a dark skin black girl was not easy or common, and it didn't give me sympathy. I cried many nights for the names people called me and how others treated me. That didn't make me weaker, though, because I didn't let it. It makes me stronger. So, if people treat me well or badly, I know how to make it work for Melvina.

I learned how to let people go and how to get the hell on. When you stick around too long, you will know. They will start yelling at you and getting in their feelings. They will exchange words that are delivered with their neck rolling and lips popping. They crack me up when they start clapping their hands when they talk and rolling their eyes. If they start cutting me off and getting rude, I start being quiet.

I don't get angry. I don't change my personality because that is beneath me. I have choices and options, and I don't have to be where they are. I can move. I normally say, "Okay, well, let me leave."

If they are at my house, it is even simpler. I go to my front door and open it. They already know what I mean. Get out. Keep reading with me; LET IT GO!

I let go of negativity, I let go of voting democratic, and I am not going to church with you. If someone has told you that you cannot let people or family go. I am here to be a living witness that, "Yes, you can."

I let a lot of people go and there isn't a person or situation that I couldn't. We have choices, and if you rob yourself of the choice, know that is still your choice. Nobody is forcing you to put up with their mess. You are choosing to put up with it.

Anyone who is toxic and got drama, or on drugs, in and out of jail, they are the bad apple in the bunch. They are going to be in another bunch, not mine. Now, for my children, they are the exception. But make no mistake, I will let go of their attitudes, and if they only want to talk to me once a year or no more, I can deal with that too. I cannot let them go and stop caring, but I can and will let go of any toxic behaviors with

Stop Overanalyzing them, for real

I raised them to have what they need. They have what they need: their own houses, cars, and phones. If all I gotta do is deal with attitudes and differences of opinions, I am good with that. Over in my heart, I am being positive and sharing love with diplomacy. I will never be their friend, I will not kiss their butts, and I will always be their mother.

My marriage also has expectations. If that were to fall apart at any time and we don't have this positive and healthy relationship because it is toxic, I can let that go too. I don't foresee that of course, but there is no one above being let go in Melvina's world! Sometimes, it is the situation you let go of. Sometimes, it is the person. Sometimes, it is how you see it, and you choose to LET IT GO.

How you spend your time is also how you choose what you let go. If you spend time with people this is how you are choosing what you want in life. Where you spend your time is what you value. If you are spending your time with people or on things you don't want to be as important in your life, you need to make some changes.

If you don't know what you want, go back to the previous chapter and make the list to figure it out. You are going to have more problems if you don't know who you are. I cannot repeat this enough because it is so easy to skip. We can think through the questions and come up with the politically correct answers and live miserably. I know I am a challenge, and I don't care.

Melvina W.

I have standards and things I want and need. I have no problem with demanding them. I have things I expect, and I want them to be respected. If a person chooses not to regard my expectations, I can move on and let it go. If you have not gotten to that point where you can or know when you should let things go, you need to read these last two chapters closely. We are almost done with this thang.

You cannot be honest with no one if you cannot be honest with things within yourself. You will miss every red flag. A red flag, I would say, is too many mistakes. If you are fifty years old and can't rub two nickels together, you have a problem. That is a big red flag. If you're gonna blame it on others, let me stop you. It's likely your children are grown, so what the hell happened?

What are you doing? Saving everyone else but letting yourself sink? While you are taking care of others, who is going to take care of you? Who is bothered by what you need? And you still feel like you need to run around with a cape on your back when you don't have anything for yourself?

How many times are you going to let someone cuss you out and treat you terribly? I mean, got dang. How long are you going to give the excuse you are their mother? Are you their correctional officer, pastor, wife, and everything else too? Let them grow up and go live how they want to and suffer the consequences. Nothing teaches us lessons faster than consequences.

You can give people chances. I believe in that. I

don't give too many chances in business, if I am honest. Second chances are not common because I realized by experience those who got the second chance still ended up fired. So, I usually skip the semantics and get it over with rather than drag it out.

As for my family, my husband and daughters get about fifty million chances. It depends on what we are talking about, but it does come with consequences. It is an intervention where you have to earn the chance and work towards it. This is not a freebie; you have to come and fight for it for me.

Make them work to keep you around. If they are not willing to work to get back to appreciate your presence, cut them off and leave them there. If you are doing it big in your business and making over a 100k a year, I doubt your best friend will be someone on Section Eight living off food stamps. If you have a doctorate, I am also sure your bestie is not someone who can't formulate a complete thought, read, or write. What are you going to have to do to nurse this relationship? Do everything for them?

We don't have time for that in life, that takes too much time, and too many are not appreciative of your time. They think people owe them something because they built their lives on others, giving them what they need to survive. I believe in being accountable, getting out here, and making it happen. Staying at home, playing games, and living off food stamps and welfare is not something I feel is the American Dream. We are in the land of opportunity, and that means going to work.

We have to work for anything we want in life,

Melvina W.

from relationships to money. There are going to be the people who won't get up to the plate to bat. Some got up to the plate and didn't perform. You gotta let them go, and you shouldn't worry about it. If they can't perform or don't appreciate you, why waste your energy to talk?

I have people I won't even speak to if they say hello to me. You wouldn't know we ever knew each other because I don't want to waste any more time or energy on people who mean no good to me. Appreciation and gratitude go hand in hand. We're moving on...

Stop Overanalyzing

There is no Perfection

You have been working hard, and I know it. It is not easy to hear things we don't want to or to change things we have been doing. I want you to know that no one is perfect, and we all have some things we need to work through and change. I am not a millionaire– yet, but I am working towards it.

I don't have all my t's crossed and i's dotted in every area of my life, but I am not giving up on what I got going on. I know where what I am putting down is appreciated, and it aligns with what I want out of life. I ain't never scared to learn something new, and I want to tell you why.

When you realize everybody puts their pants on one leg at a time like you, there isn't much difference between people. Yes money is a difference, but if I got the same will they have, I can make more. If I have the same desire to win, no matter where I am starting, I know I can have more. If you have a no-fail personality and mindset, you will have more, no matter what that looks like.

Not all of us will be billionaires or millionaires, but we can be! If you look at how much money runs through your hands during a lifetime you will see that you had over a million dollars, but how did you spend it? Did you buy whole life insurance so you can retire one day? Did you put things in place to make your life easier, or did you come up with excuses and delay what you needed to do?

If you have delayed making these decisions, it is not over. I didn't say it was over, but you are getting a late start. You might have to double down on some things to help redeem some of the time lost, and some things are just passed over. You can't go backward and fix everything. Sometimes, you have to pick up where you are and keep it moving.

You have to let some things go because not everything needs a second look, second opinion, or more of your time. Don't think that your time has no value because of how it looks now. I used to be broke as a joke. When I was sitting on the couch with my lights turned out, I had the same value I got today. I was the same Melvina, but I had to make changes to get here. I had to grow and not be afraid to take the limits off my life.

For some of us, we are afraid to leave people behind. We are afraid of what people will think if we say no. We are afraid of how our children will treat us if we don't give them what they want when they want it.

There Is No Perfection

We are out here fixing everybody else's life while ours comes crumbling down.

You have to decide you are not going to do this. You have to make the decision to do better and not be stuck on things that won't benefit you. You have to become your number one fan because everyone will not make the train. You are going to have to leave some people behind. You are going to have to leave some situations behind. You can't solve every problem, and for some things, the best solution is to let it the fuck go!

I mean that because we can hold onto people and things that will keep us stuck. If you feel stuck in life, that is because you are holding on to someone or something you haven't decided to let go. Maybe it is not the person or thing, maybe it is you? Maybe you are the reason why you keep going in the same circle.

If you realize you have a problem and you are in denial about it, it is time to wake up and let the excuses go! You are living one life, and if you are wasting your time you are going to regret that later. We don't get younger. Things change, and so can you. You don't have to be the same mother you were to your children at two years old at thirty-two years old.

Let people grow up and become responsible. Stop letting them suck on your titty and push them out of your lap! They are grown, and you deserve to enjoy your life. Stop allowing your children to sabotage your relationships. You better not allow your children to keep you single because they are all going to leave you one day. You are going to be the lonely one, and they might

Melvina W.

not come and visit you!

For the ones with your children still in the house who are disrespectful, make them get out. Or make them accountable if they stay. They have to have a job and a plan to get out in 6 months. If they can't figure it out, put them out. Some of our children will have an excuse for why they cannot, no matter the circumstances. If they have time to smoke drugs, have girlfriends, or boyfriends, they have time to get a second job and take care of themselves.

Stop putting up with the mess and expect to be blessed. I am not religious, but I see the writing on the wall. Nothing good comes from allowing people to crap on your doorstep. Taking crap off other people doesn't make you have a better day, it means your day stinks! Why should you keep living like that when they can sleep at night?

Why are you upset about their situation and life choices when they are not bothered? You need to stop caring more than they do. If they say, "Woe is me, and I can't," agree with them and move on. I don't sit up here and argue with nobody about how they feel or what they choose to do with their lives. I let them get on the train, and if they want to jump from a cliff, I will let them.

If I love them, I will try to step in front of them and ask questions, but if they are pushing past me and gun-ho on going forward, what can I do? Sit around and watch? No. It hurt to see my brother make choices that led him to an early grave. I loved him, but I couldn't do

There Is No Perfection

much else to save him or change his ways.

The choices he made, he had to live with, and ultimately, I did too, as did the rest of my family. We will have to live with the choices other people make, and we cannot save them. We cannot save anyone who doesn't want to be saved or helped. I threw out lifelines, but he didn't pick up one of them.

You cannot live for someone else. You can only live for you and teach others how to live for them. I raised three daughters who can take care of themselves. No matter what happens in life, they know what to do. I am grateful that Glenn and I did that together. We were a team, and no, we didn't get it all right, but we did our best. We gave them all we had.

They didn't want for nothing. They got cars, phones, games, clothes, food, and all the love we have. If that wasn't enough for them, well that is just too bad. I am not going to be over here crying my eyes out because my children didn't appreciate me. I will not stand at the door knocking forever to be let in. I will see my position in their lives and will let go of what is out of my control.

I will not stop being me. I will not stop being their mother. I will be that to the day they die. I love my children, and there are people I love, too. People who you want to save, but you will not be able to make them do something they don't choose to do. So what can you do? Do you hear my question what can you do? Be boo boo the fool? Hmmm?

Melvina W.

You can teach them what you know. You can encourage them to grow up. You can help guide them when they ask for your help. You can be a support, but you are not taking responsibility for how grown people choose to live their lives. You are not subject to their demands, you make your own choices.

What you can change? What you want to do? What you need to do, do that first. What is out of your control or is working as a distraction for you, let it go. Some things are not worth your time, and you are the one who decides what that is. I am glad you took the time to read this book and enjoy my collection of three books: Come Hell or High Water, I Didn't Say It Was Over, and Let It Go! I have a special message and gift for you when you scan the QR code.

Also, if you haven't read all three books, get them. My journey will encourage you and help you know that you can do this. I am a medical coding mentor, I have a school, and if you want to get into this business, I can help you. My process works; it is affordable, and no, it is not free. Nothing I have right now did I get for free. I worked for it and I spent the money that was necessary to get it done. I want you to do the same thing I did to change my life to go from robbing Peter

There Is No Perfection
to pay Paul, to where I am now.

So, I have something free I can give you, it's not the program, because I don't want money to be the reason you don't move forward today in this business or life. So scan this QR and connect with me to get what I am giving. It doesn't happen too often because I like money, but I love people.

Lastly, I want you to stay connected with me and grow with me. I want to see you get the job you want and advance in life. So, I started a podcast to help you on the way called Give Me Something to Work With QR. This show is about being a woman, a wife, a mother, a medical coder, author, and a business owner. I share my perspective, and many people find me provocative and entertaining. So come and press play at IAmMelvinaPodcast.com

Melvina W.
I want to leave you with a few lasting words:

Melvina's Thoughts:
Do you have the thought process of being stuck? Let It Go… and figure it out. Don't make an excuse, instead make a plan, make a goal…

Melvina's Thoughts:
Do you feel like you are not worthy of success or that it is never going to happen for you? If so, Let It Go…get rid of that thought process, and know that you are enough! Believe and know there is ONLY one you. There is no life without YOU. You are valuable, and you are enough!

Melvina's words to live by… Make these words yours

I don't have to be perfect.
I am always growing and evolving.
I have weaknesses.
I can't please everyone.
I don't have to know everything.
I can say "NO" and NOT feel guilty.
I'm doing what's best for ME.
I make mistakes.
It's safe for me to UNAPOLOGETICALLY be me!

Welp, this train is leaving, and I gotta go. See you soon, bye for now.

There Is No Perfection

About the Author

Melvina W is a firm believer in Infinite Possibilities! She was born and raised in Savannah, Georgia, and more than exemplifies the true meaning of going above and beyond, believing the sky is the limit.

Melvina has more than 15 years of expertise in the Health Information Management (HIM) arena. She has worked for several hospitals across the United States, from Level One to Four, Teaching facilities, Trauma and Critical care units, and many more. She specializes in several medical coding disciplines.

Melvina also acquired a passion for coding and auditing charts for several Professional Service disciplines such as Inpatient, Observations, Consults, Clinics, and more. Melvina is infatuated with validating all coding assignments, modifiers, and diagnoses to ensure compliance with the HIM arena, and she loves solving "HIM problematic edits for Federal, State, and payer-specific regulations. Melvina has proven to be a person who collaborates with physicians to improve documentation to obtain the utmost reimbursement

About Melvina Washington

for the healthcare facility. In addition to coding, auditing, and compliance assignments, she is an excellent communicator, motivator, and team player who fully completes her projects and assignments with the highest confidentiality and accuracy possible.

In addition to her work, Melvina is the owner/founder and President of Infinity Health Information Management (HIM) and Infinity HIM School, where she has implemented an eight-week medical coding program for any potential persons who would like to break into the coding field. Melvina is changing the paradigm by teaching medical coding by focusing on a specific type of coding to create subject matter experts for faster turnaround of employment for the students.

Melvina has employed and assisted her students in gaining experience and advanced knowledge of the coding world. She offers training, education, resume assistance and interviewing techniques, consulting, and even job placement to qualified persons to gain real-world experience!

Melvina has a Master's in Business Administration with a concentration in Healthcare Management, a Bachelor's in Computer Information Systems, and an Associate's degree in Health Information Technology from the University of Phoenix. She is a Registered Health Information Technician (RHIT) with the American Health Information Management Association (AHIMA). She is also a Certified Professional Coder (CPC) with the American Academy of Professional Coders (AAPC). Melvina is a Georgia American Health Information Management Association (GAHIMA) and AAPC member. Attending meetings and networking with these organizations has enabled Melvina to correspond with other leaders in the industry and better coach her students.

Melvina has been a proud member of Zeta Phi Beta Sorority, Incorporated, since 2014 and has

remained a member of Sigma Mu Zeta Chapter since her induction. She has been highly active within her chapter and volunteers in various community programs. Melvina believes in the power of giving back and placed 5th for all regions for March of Dimes under the Zeta Phi Beta Inc. individual fundraiser in 2019 and first place in 2020. She is a major contributor for the American Cancer Society, serves people experiencing homelessness, and plays bingo with seniors at nursing homes, among other activities.

In addition, Melvina owns the Infinite Beauty Blog and Black Cup of Joe platforms. Both blogs encourage women to chase their dreams and buy products and services to help make their lives and communities better. Melvina says, "I am blessed and fortunate," she feels she needs to share her story with other women looking for guidance to start or grow a business. She wrote and published her first book,

About Melvina Washington Come Hell or High Water, and created a course for a deeper study.

Melvina has been happily married to Glenn Feaster for 26 years and resides in Georgia. They are proud parents of three daughters who have graduated Historically Black Colleges/Universities. The oldest daughter, Mariama Aisha is working as a Meteorologist. She has her Masters and Bachelors degree and she is also a member of Zeta Phi Beta, Inc.

The twins, Sierra Leone is working as a Special Education Teacher has her Bachelor's degree and attending school for her Masters degree and Amira Nkeiruka is working as a Civil Engineer has her bachelor's degree.

Melvina W.

Her three daughters are pursuing their dreams using the strong foundation Melvina and Glenn have implemented. Melvina's family is well-traveled. They have visited Canada, Mexico, France, Turkey, Italy, the United Kingdom, Egypt, Ghana, Togo, Australia, New Zealand, the Caribbean Islands, Columbia, and over 30 States in the US so far.

Melvina's words to live by:

> "Do not be afraid of changing the paradigm. Make your own rules and follow them. Aggressively obtain financial education and wealth to leave a more secure, stabilized infrastructure for your family lineage. Believe that education creates options so you don't become complacent with your career or life. Expect the best; however, always have a backup plan and expect the unexpected. Remember always to give back, help others grow, and develop into what you have already come; pass it forward."

"Be yourself, dream big, work hard, play harder, and believe in infinite possibilities."

Melvina W., MBA, RHIT, CPC Owner/President of Infinity HIM School, Infinite Beauty Possibilities, Black Cup of Joe Organizer, and Published Author/Mentor

Website: Infinityhim.com
Website: infinityhimschool.com
Website: jobinfinityhim.com
Website: IAmMelvina.com
Website: IAMMelvinaW.com
Website: IAmMelvinaPodcast.com

About Melvina Washington
Website: BlackCupofJoe.com
Website: InfiniteBeauty.blog

Email:
infinity@infinityhim.com or info@Iammelvina.com

SCAN ME

Call or Text:
770-240-0089 Press Extension 1
Web: KLEpub.com
Email Services@klepub.com

It's time to start and finish **YOUR Story!**

KLE Publishing specializes in helping people become authors. In as little as 15 to 90 days, we can help you develop your books and e-books and publish to 39,000 outlets! We also offer audiobook services.

Write, Edit, Format, Publish
We can help from
Start to Finish.

Explore and learn more about published authors affiliated with KLE.

  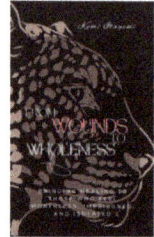  
 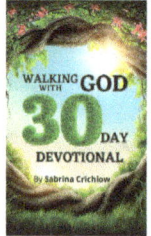   

KLEPub.com

SCAN ME
Or Use Link

Connect with KLE

Services to Launch or Grow Your Business for Authors & Product or Service based Companies

TURN
Key SOlution

Four Departments:
- Coaching and Consulting - Business SWOT Analysis
- Writing and Publishing Dept: Writing Services, Book/Ebook/Audio Book Services
- Business Concierge: Social Media, Web, CRM, and New Business Formulation Support: Message, Brand, Sales, Product Development, Strategy
- Production: Content Creation

www.ingramcontent.com/pod-product-compliance
Lightning Source LLC
Chambersburg PA
CBHW061758070526
44586CB00023B/2620